SAILING FOR SEALS

SAILING FOR SEALS

Jenny Hobson

Published by Jennifer Hobson

Any omissions, inaccuracies or errors are entirely down to the author.

Some names of people and boats have been changed to preserve anonymity.

All photographs by Jenny and Richard Hobson unless otherwise credited.

All wildlife photographs were taken with a telephoto lens with no disturbance to the subjects.

Front cover campaign seal logo: artwork by Lorraine Auton, designer Tony Colledge

A CIP catalogue record for this book is available from the British Library.

ISBN 978-1-7390837-0-0

Book layout and cover design by Clare Brayshaw

Prepared and printed by:

York Publishing Services Ltd
64 Hallfield Road
Layerthorpe
York YO31 7ZQ

Tel: 01904 431213

Website: www.yps-publishing.co.uk

Dedication

This book is dedicated to the grey seal Pinkafo and to all
the people who strive with passion and dedication
to protect seals from disturbance and entanglement.

50% of the profits from this book will be donated to
Friends of Horsey Seals and
RSPCA East Winch Wildlife Centre

Contents

The Author

Jenny Hobson took up sailing later in life initially learning how to sail dinghies on inland waters before progressing to coastal sailing on larger boats. She worked through the RYA sailing qualifications from competent crew to day skipper and yacht master. Sailing has been one of her main activities ever since.

In 2009 she moved to Norfolk and started to volunteer for a RSPCA Wildlife Centre helping to care for seals and a range of other animals and birds.

In 2019 she initiated the awareness campaign, 'Love Seals – keeping seals safe from plastic flying rings', with the support of the charity Friends of Horsey Seals, after experiencing firsthand the horrific injuries caused to these beautiful animals by entanglement in discarded plastic rings.

Her husband's early retirement in April 2022 allowed them to fulfil a long held ambition to set off on an extended cruise around the UK.

Foreword

They sailed away for six months and a day...
(with apologies to Edward Lear)

Essentially *Sailing for Seals* is a diary, but it's also a hymn to Jenny Hobson's passion for wildlife, and the love of sailing that she shares with her husband, Richard.

Sailing for Seals is a book that tells the story of how Jenny and Richard combined those passions to achieve a long-held sailing ambition, and to spread awareness of a campaign to help save the lives of seals around UK shores.

While Richard laboured on, Jenny, taking retirement earlier, was able to volunteer at the RSPCA's Wildlife Centre at East Winch, not far from King's Lynn and their home in a delightful West Norfolk village.

The Wildlife Centre is an extraordinary place, equipped with interior and outdoor facilities that include pools suitable to accommodate and aid the recovery of sick and injured seals. Not only are its facilities remarkable, but so are the veterinary skills and expertise employed there; and the dedication and care given by the staff of wildlife assistants and volunteers who look after the array of mini and mighty patients taken in to be made whole again.

A few years ago Jenny was among the first to witness the wounds on the neck of a seal that was encircled by a plastic throwing ring. This animal was a young adult female Atlantic grey seal, which as a pup had pushed her head through the hollow centre, suffering deep lacerations from its sharp edges as she grew.

The veterinary and nursing staff that received this animal, rescued from certain death by trained seal handlers from the charity Friends of Horsey Seals, were aghast at the extent of her injury. They had little expectation of a good outcome. But grey seals are made of strong stuff, and so is the caring team at East Winch. Among them was Jenny.

All gave their finest efforts to keep that patient alive. They could see that such injuries could be avoided if people knew what can happen if toys like this, indeed any plastic item that can be investigated and get entangled around the neck of a seal pup in this way, find their way into the sea. Jenny made up her mind that something had to be done to stop this unintended cruelty and the birth of the *'Flying Rings Campaign'* to save seal lives was forged.

In 2019 Jenny approached me to help with the development of an information leaflet for use in the campaign and Peter Ansell BEM, Chair of Friends of Horsey Seals, officially launched the campaign in July of that year.

Since then Jenny's drive and enthusiasm has achieved press and media coverage locally and nationally thanks to her devotion and that of willing volunteers to help make known this potential threat to wildlife. Jenny's determination knows no bounds in getting increased legal protection of seals to take this danger into consideration.

Meanwhile, Richard worked, they sailed together whenever opportunities arose, and both continued to plan for the day when Richard would be free and they would weigh anchor and start their voyage.

The account of that voyage in *Sailing for Seals* is personal, poetic, educational, part travelogue, and sometimes comic. Jenny's account gives you the smell of sea breezes and the sound of storms through the rigging that were part of their six months voyage.

You can share the delight that Jenny and her sister, Phil, enjoyed on a wildlife-watching safari on the Isle of Mull; pick up sailing terms you might not know; and learn, should you need it, how to surmount the tricky task of raising and lowering a 9 tonne, 36ft long boat through a series of locks to traverse the Crinan and Caledonian Canals.

Written without hyperbole, Jenny's love of nature shows in her descriptions of seeing marine mammals and birds on the voyage and walking in woodland and mountains that mark a boundary between coast and countryside. Accompany her and Richard as they visit the small towns and villages clustered around the many ports they visit. Discover with them some of the fascinating histories they uncover.

Together both partners enjoyed company and conversations with people they met en route locally, and with fellow sailors. Jenny made new acquaintances in her dealings with business owners of seaside stores as she raised their awareness to the plight of injured seals

As for the campaign, someone who can plan and carry out a voyage like this one can clearly take other things in their stride. With an onboard media interview and campaign volunteers following a strategy agreed before Jenny's departure, no impetus was lost and good news awaited on her return.

I've lived the voyage through Jenny's words, hearing her voice telling the story, and I feel as if I was there too. I hope you enjoy reading *Sailing for Seals* just as much as I have.

Albert Ward

Trustee, Friends of Horsey Seals

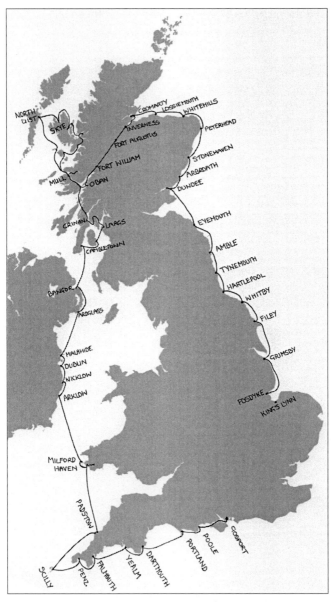

Spirit's sailing track

Setting the Scene

I'll start with a true story.

One cold dark December evening in 2018, I was volunteering at the RSPCA Wildlife Centre in East Winch in Norfolk, when an adult grey seal was brought in with a pink flying ring (a frisbee with a hole in the centre) deeply embedded into her neck. She was the second seal to be rescued and brought to the East Winch Centre caught in a plastic ring, the first being another adult female grey seal who was named Frisbee. It was evident that Frisbee's plight was not a freak occurrence.

Pinkafo, as she was later nicknamed due to the colour of the ring, was at death's door: the wounds caused by the ring had become infected and she was starving. I don't know if it was because I saw her just as she arrived, with the ring in place and the harm it had caused, but my heart broke and I felt in that split second I had to do something to stop this happening to other seals.

The following January I went to see Peter Ansell who had brought Pinkafo in and is Chair of Friends of Horsey Seals (FoHS), a Norfolk charity which protects seals on the Norfolk coast. We talked as we strolled along Horsey beach and I asked Peter if the group would support an awareness campaign to tell people about the dangers of plastic flying rings to seals and how everyone can help. The group gladly agreed and the campaign started to form. We would build on the media coverage that the East Winch manager had gained showing the plight of Frisbee and Pinkafo.

During that beach walk Peter and I saw a large group of grey seals resting on the beach; on the far side near to the sea, lay an adult seal with a yellow flying ring caught around its neck. I felt so sad to see yet another entangled seal.

Three years on, the campaign had gathered momentum with growing awareness in East Anglia, support from coastal councils and good media coverage. Many shop owners selling beach toys had taken flying rings off their shelves, though not all. An increasing number of seals had been spotted on the Norfolk coast caught in flying rings and in 2021 the Cornwall Seal Research Trust spotted another two caught in plastic rings on the Cornish coast. Thankfully both these seals were eventually caught and their rings removed by British Divers Marine Life Rescue (BDMLR).

In 2022 my husband Richard retired and it seemed like a great opportunity to combine our plan to sail around the country with promoting the campaign nationally.

I wrote a private weekly blog during our voyage, mainly to keep in touch with family and friends, and as a record of our trip. Based on the blog, this book highlights our adventures, life on board a sailing boat, the wildlife we saw and how, on the way, we sailed for seals.

Jenny Hobson, January 1st 2023

1

Countdown, Final Preparation and Off!

JANUARY 1ST, 2022

After years of dreaming, planning and saving we were finally preparing to swap living ashore for life afloat on our 11 metre long (36 foot) yacht Spirit of Space, to go sailing for 6 months. Our plan was to cast off in April on a clockwise voyage around the country starting from Gosport in Portsmouth Harbour, where our boat was berthed, bound for Fosdyke Yacht Haven, a tiny boatyard 40 minutes from home on the River Welland in Lincolnshire. During this passage, we hoped to visit some of the best cruising grounds around the UK including the Isles of Scilly, the east coast of Ireland and the Islands and Highlands of Scotland's west coast, before returning down the east coast to the Wash.

Spirit of Space is a Rustler 36, a modern boat of classical design by Holman & Pye, with a well proven record for offshore cruising. Although not having the plentiful accommodation of more modern designs of the same length, the boat has an easy motion when at sea and is designed for extended passage making whilst keeping her crew comfortable and safe. Another attribute which we find very important is that she is breathtakingly beautiful for the eye to behold. We never tire of looking back at her sleek and powerful lines when dinghying ashore. Her sail plan, a Bermudan rig, consists of a large furling genoa (the front sail) and a smaller mainsail, both of which are controlled from the cockpit. Spirit's long keel lying under the water provides safety and stability. Of her nine metric tonnes, almost half is from lead encapsulated within the bottom third of her keel. This means she will right herself quickly from extreme angles if pushed over by wind or waves.

To ensure we both keep sharp and practiced in our navigation and passage planning skills, we alternate taking the responsibility of skipper each year. The payoff of being skipper is getting to choose our sailing destinations. As it fell that I would be skipper for our first year of extended cruising, the choice of route and sailing for the seals was mine.

We prepared our boat following a critical path analysis (CPA) as long as your arm, which listed all the jobs needed, as well as allocating specific completion dates. This caused Richard a huge amount of work and stress as Chief Engineer. However, our efforts resulted in a re-rig, changing the metal wires that hold up the mast, and buying a new cruising chute (a large downwind sail) which I hoped would be one of the keys to promoting the seal flying rings campaign: but it was huge and we didn't know where we were going to store it! We had also bought and read a pilot book for the east coast and the Wash to see if we could actually navigate into Fosdyke with our deep draft yacht. By the end of December there were 43 more jobs on the boat CPA to do and I also had my own list of house and garden tasks to complete.

Spirit of Space our home for six months

*Spirit's interior clockwise from top left: saloon, galley,
chart table and forepeak bunk*

Richard was 100 percent looking forward to life afloat and doing boat jobs in beautiful locations. With some trepidation I was also looking forward to letting go of my daily routines, exploring new places and experiencing wildlife both on land and at sea.

One of a sailor's worst fears is water getting into their boat. When we returned to Gosport at the start of April for a final week of essential jobs on Spirit we found the bilge (the sump at the bottom of the boat where water collects) was full of fresh water. After pumping it out we discovered that the metal water tank was empty and we both spent the night worrying that it had sprung a leak. We could not have set off if this was the case. Luckily Richard diagnosed the problem as a leaky valve from the calorifier (the hot water tank). With the offending tap washer reversed it was secure and we refilled the main fresh water tank – a top tip if you cannot find a spare tap washer!

The last few weeks of getting ready were frenetic, we could not believe how much work there was in prepping the boat and leaving our home for six months. I alone had over 30 jobs on my boat and house list, from servicing lifejackets and buying an updated electronic chart, to organising accounts, buying bird food to last for the duration, provisioning, fitting plant waterers, organising post, choosing house key holders and saying au revoir to friends.

Richard retired from work after 40 years in the newspaper industry on Friday April 1st. He travelled to Germany that last week to his company head office and enjoyed send-off celebrations there and also at his local base in King's Lynn.

We made the final five-hour drive to Gosport to complete the essential jobs on Spirit, then returned home for one last day before taking the train down to Portsmouth, as we could not leave a car down there, at last we were finally free.

Why the rush? We had been watching the weather and it looked as if we would get favourable winds to go west. I think we just wanted to get going as well, aware that without a deadline we would faff and prevaricate. On Tuesday April 12th we cast off from our berth in Gosport which had been Spirit's home for six years.

We both had our own expectations of what it would be like beginning a sailing life for six months – how different reality can be! Richard's vision of a calm, sunny sail wearing shorts and t-shirt dissolved as, after a calm start, the wind shifted sooner than expected and we found ourselves beating (sailing close into the wind) against a brisk southwesterly trying to get out of the Solent. We needed to reef the mainsail and found the first reefing line had become undone, then the furling system to reduce the genoa (the large front sail) stuck, worryingly. The wind was increasing and the sail and its lines were whipping around the foredeck. Finally Richard noticed the problem: a furling block positioned the wrong way round during our re-rig. He turned it around and, with relief, we managed to reduce sail and made our way more comfortably out of the Solent into Poole Bay, where we took turns to collapse below for a rest. I lay cold and miserable missing my warm comfy sofa at home, friends and activities and thought "This is only day one, with 170 to go!"

We spent our first night attached to an eco mooring buoy in beautiful Studland Bay. This type of buoy is secured to the sea bed by a single helical screw minimising disturbance, in this case, to protect the sea horses and their eel grass habitats. The night was windy, noisy and a bit uncomfortable with Spirit rocking in the swell but in the morning all was calm and peaceful. The iconic wooden pilot cutter Jolie Brise (she won the inaugural Fastnet race in 1925) was moored near us, a good omen we felt.

Thankfully, our next sail west onto Portland Harbour was problem free and we anchored there to the noisy sound of chattering terns above. Across the harbour however an ominous bank of grey sea fog descended over the Isle of Portland, folding over the prison and gradually extending to cover us all.

I had made a passage plan for us to take the notorious inshore route around Portland Bill, where the tides run strongly for 10 out of 12 hours and you risk the horrors of the race, dangerous water, if you stray too far offshore; thinking we would likely be fogbound and unable to leave. In the morning though, the fog had lifted off most of the harbour and visibility was improving. My plan worked and with eagle eyes looking out for lobster pot floats submerged by the racing tide, we passed safely round the Bill close enough to throw a biscuit to the shore.

The fog cloaked us in varying degrees right across Lyme Bay with no wind to blow it away and forcing us to use our engine. As we neared Dartmouth, our destination, with its promise of rest and shore leave, the fog thickened so much we could not see the entrance to the river. Luckily or understandably, we could tell no other boats were about by using our radar and AIS (Automatic Identification System), and our chart plotter helped us buoy-hop our way in. At last the trees and banks magically revealed themselves, we were safe. A little motorboat chugged passed us towards the bank of fog then, thinking better of it, hurriedly scurried back for home.

The fog lifting in Dartmouth entrance

Moored on a river pontoon we could finally enjoy some of our vision: steam trains and river life in the beautiful Dart Valley.

2

Highlights of Dartmouth, Falmouth and Penzance

APRIL 14TH, 2022

As a sailor in Dartmouth, you can stay in one of the three marinas or rough it on a river pontoon with no shore power or water. We always choose the latter as it puts us in the middle of life on the river: steam trains to watch on the Kingswear side, river boats chugging up to Dittisham and Totnes past the novelist Agatha Christie's house Greenways. There is also plenty of wildlife to observe and enjoy.

Dartmouth is steeped in history with scenery and architecture to match. Thomas Newcomen, inventor of the first practical beam steam engine, was born here in 1664: you can see an actual preserved engine working in the tourist information centre. Steam trains chuff regularly up to Paignton and back on the Kingswear side of the river, making a spectacular backdrop to our pontoon whilst the river entrance is flanked by two pretty 14th century castles. The historic ship Mayflower set sail from Dartmouth bound for the New World in 1620, with the Pilgrim Fathers on board. Bayards Cove is an incredibly well preserved quayside, which provided one of the main sets for The Onedin Line TV series. A fascinating attraction is the tiny Kingswear passenger cum car ferry; originally a rowing boat in the 1700s, it is now operated by a powerful little tug which pivots on the bow to change direction and push its cargo from one side of the river to the other.

From our river pontoon we needed to inflate our dinghy to reach the town. En route we saw a grey seal several times mooching around the river and once chomping on a flat fish it had just caught. The seal was relaxed and confident in its natural habitat, a stark contrast to Pinkafo when she was brought into the RSPCA Wildlife Centre that December evening, with the plastic flying ring embedded around her neck. I remembered how the vet had had to cut the ring off with secateurs. She was then treated with antibiotics and pain killers, and put in a shallow salt bath to help heal her wounds. It was touch and go whether she would survive her first night but amazingly she did and started, we hoped, on the slow road to recovery.

Pinkafo, the ring is chipped but intact (Photo credit FoHS)

Pinkafo before her rescue, near death (Photo credit FoHS)

Exploring ashore, we followed a secret path above the estuary through woods deep with spring flowers, celandine, dog violets, green alkanet and herb robert, up to Gallants Bower, the site of a stronghold which was fortified by Royalists in the 1600s. The beauty of the site is its tranquillity, stupendous views over the estuary and swathes of bluebell and primrose.

One of the differences we began to notice between living aboard rather than being on holiday was developing our IT skills. I had been somewhat resistant to embracing smart phones and tablets but actually learnt quickly how to produce a blog, download films, i-sounds and audio books for information and entertainment. As a consequence, we both began to look out for free Wi-Fi and found this in the local sailing club, where we spent several hours for the price of hot drinks and snacks.

Since leaving our permanent berth in Gosport and the benefits of being plugged into the 240v shore power, we had noticed that the fridge kept trying to start but the compressor would not run. Also, after a couple of nights mid-river in Dartmouth on just battery power the diesel heating would not fire up, even though there was plenty of charge showing in the domestic batteries. It was time for the Chief Engineer, aka Richard, to break out the multimeter.

Although we were showing a standing voltage of 12.4v across the battery terminal posts, only 11.3v was reaching the fridge compressor terminals. This was a sure sign of voltage drop somewhere in the system. Extending the negative lead on the multimeter allowed the Chief Engineer to point test the system voltage across all the connections in the chain, from the battery through to the fridge. The culprit was identified as the main domestic 80 amp fuse; it had not blown but was restricting the flow of current. As the Chief Engineer carries enough spares onboard to build a second boat(!) he had one of these to hand and the fridge was happily up and running again.

After four days enjoying Dartmouth we set sail in calm weather heading west for an overnight stop on the River Yealm close to the Plymouth estuary. The river has a sand bank extending across its entrance leaving a narrow gap marked by buoys. Shallow water to Misery Point just beyond the bank meant we needed to anchor on the outside of the entrance in Wembury Bay until the tide had flooded to a safe height. Richard slept while I kept watch. We then followed the marked channel past the sandbank and up the river turning Spirit into the racing flood tide to pick up a visitor mooring buoy. That night we stayed on board enjoying a beautiful sunset and the sight of two kayakers silhouetted against the evening light.

The weather continued fair next day with such a light northwesterly wind we ended up motor sailing most of the eight-hour, 40-mile passage to Falmouth. We were welcomed by Falmouth Marina and given five free visitor nights as we had plenty of visitor credits left on our account. We were able to use these in lieu of payment as Falmouth and Gosport are part of the same marina group.

That first evening, we stretched our land legs by walking to the little town of Penryn, further up the river of the same name. Hearing church bells ringing, we followed their peals and discovered ringers practising at St Gluvia's. We showed our appreciation and the leader invited us in to listen and watch. It was an uplifting experience to hear the bells and fascinating to understand about some of the basic techniques of bell ringing and the connections between bell ringing groups. We then went in search of fish, veggie burger and chips which we enjoyed eating in the quiet of the Rotary Remembrance Garden which commemorates 18 lives that were lost when The Square, next to the garden, was bombed during the Second World War.

Falmouth provided a welcome interlude helping us to slow down and adjust to our new cruising life. Our idea had always been to savour the journey, take up opportunities and relax into exploring wherever we land. The town of Falmouth is steeped in sailing history and wandering along its ancient streets, catching glimpses of the harbour at the end of the snickets, we caught a flavour of the past. It is easy to visualise square rigged ships making their first landfall here after an Atlantic crossing and waiting for orders for their next port of discharge to unload their goods. In the town's Art Gallery we stumbled upon a quirky exhibition of automata, clock-work models with moving parts and figures, and on the Friday before we left I did a beach clean on Gyllynvase beach for Earth Day.

We found one shop on the High Street which was selling flying rings. I took the opportunity to explain to the shop assistants how young seals find lost or discarded rings in the sea and being intelligent, highly inquisitive mammals, they play with them sometimes putting their head through the hole in the middle. Once entangled they can't get them off as they have flippers not arms like us and all their movement is forward. As they grow bigger and bigger into adults, the ring cuts into their neck causing the most horrendous wounds which sadly, will eventually kill them. The assistants were very concerned for the seals and promised to pass the message and a campaign leaflet on to the owner.

*

I was quite used to talking to people about the seals and the campaign after three years of practice and was reminded of how it all started and how the publicity I was giving out had evolved. Driving back from visiting Peter on Horsey beach back in January

2019, my mind had been racing with ideas of how to get a simple message across to all the people who visit the beautiful, sandy beaches of Norfolk. Images seemed the obvious way of showing how the seals were getting entangled together with a plea for positive action: 'Please take your flying rings home'. But, this was the first campaign I had been involved in and I was starting from scratch. I researched how to put a message across, finding a treasure trove of ideas in the Framing Nature Toolkit, (a guide by the Public Interest Research Centre), and the Futerra website which told me: 'People will protect nature because they want to not because they have to'.

The distressing photos of the seals needed to be reframed into an image that showed the problem without putting people off. I had approached a local wildlife artist Lorraine Auton who agreed to paint a friendly, engaging image of a young seal with a flying ring around its neck for the centrepiece of a poster. Her partner Tony was happy to carry out the design work. I also spent an afternoon pouring over the design of a leaflet with Albert from FoHS. Eventually, the publicity was produced with the positive title 'Love Seals?' It contained stories of rescued seals and upbeat messages about how everyone could help including: 'Please take your flying rings home'.

I prepared a funding application to Sea-Changers with the help of Hilda, the fund raiser for FoHS, and we were awarded a grant to produce publicity and promote the campaign. This success boosted my confidence and involved preparing a detailed plan which gave an invaluable structure of aims and activities. We sought the support of other organisations whose logos could be displayed along with FoHS and Sea-Changers including the RSPCA, BDMLR (British Divers Marine Life Rescue), and Marine Life Rescue – another Norfolk seal rescue charity.

On April 2nd 2019 the FoHS rescue team had managed to catch a third adult grey seal which had a yellow flying ring embedded into his neck. It is only when seals become very ill and incapacitated that it is possible to rescue them, and this male seal was weak and emaciated. He was named Sir David by the RSPCA when he was admitted to the East Winch Centre after the famous naturalist Sir David Attenborough, and was included as one of the seal stories in our campaign leaflet. I hoped this was the same seal that I had seen on Horsey beach when walking with Peter.

*

In Falmouth Marina, we were berthed next to a merry pair of spaniels who lived aboard a pretty wooden boat with their owners. We heard the younger one squealing with anticipation and delight whenever shore leave was mentioned – this occurred at least twice a day, the first being shortly after dawn! The day before our departure the dogs were being taken for their daily exercise when we saw them stop in their tracks on the pontoon. Approaching from the opposite direction was a person holding a long lead with something small, beige, and furry at the end of it contained in a harness. It was a ferret! Taking the ferret for a walk seemed to be perfectly natural for the owner but it was the strangest thing we had ever seen.

So it was with the help of the dawn doggy call, we woke in good time to set sail on April 25th for Penzance. We had fuelled up and taken on water as these would become more difficult to access on our journey westward.

We had a cracking sail with real waves along the Lizard peninsula, which extends to the south from Falmouth. The wind as forecasted was an east-southeasterly force 3-5 on the Beaufort Scale (8 – 24 mph) and we achieved a speed of six knots sometimes seven which is Spirit's fastest hull speed. My passage plan worked true, we had tide with us all the way, which took us round Lizard Point arriving at Penzance Harbour just before high water.

With the wind on our quarter we needed to gybe (passing the stern of the yacht through the wind) to cross Mount's Bay towards Penzance. This manoeuvre needs to be carried out with care: when the wind gets behind the mainsail it whips the sail and its metal supporting boom across the boat at an alarming and dangerous rate, with a sharp crack. The effect of this is greatly reduced by drawing the sail into the centre of the boat so it can hardly move as the wind takes it. The sail can then be let out safely on the other side. A top tip we learnt from the legendary skipper Tom Cunliffe is to leave the genoa until the main is gybed, then the genoa can be drawn through without drama.

The skipper helming across to Scilly

Like Falmouth, Penzance Harbour harks back to an earlier age. No marina this, rather a working dock which thankfully welcomes leisure boaters like us. Rafted up against other vessels, we needed to be agile to climb across them and scale ladders up the harbour walls. Tired and hungry, we found a cheap all-day breakfast in town then fell into our bunk to nap.

On awaking later that evening we chatted to our neighbours in Blue Mallow who had sailed down from Portishead and were bound for Seville. Next to them was the Jorgen Amundsen, a Norwegian working ship registered in Panama, which we all had to climb across to get ashore. During the night the De Gallant arrived, a Dutch wooden eco-trading sailing schooner. It was a truly international gathering of boats and sailors.

The following morning we found The Quirky Bird a friendly, down-to-earth café with free Wi-Fi, just what we needed to publish our weekly blog and catch up on admin whilst enjoying rolls and hot drinks. I opened an email from a seal supporter called Kate Wing. Kate had found and photographed an adult seal on Pakefield beach in Suffolk that had died from being caught in a plastic flying ring. She was so deeply saddened that she started a government petition to call for a ban on the rings. Kate included a link for the petition and I immediately forwarded it on to all my contacts.

Whilst in Penzance I also caught up with Sue Sayer of the Seal Research Trust in Cornwall. Sue and her group have supported the campaign from the start and were launching their own following the sightings of two seals in 2021 off the west coast caught in flying rings.

We realized that to reach our next destination, the Isles of Scilly, in daylight, we could not leave from Penzance as access in and out of the harbour is restricted to just before and after high water, which was around 2pm. The only all-tide harbour close by was Newlyn, home to one of the largest fishing fleets in the Southwest and, as rumour had it, not overly welcoming to yachts. Happily, the Penzance harbourmaster rang Newlyn for us and booked us in for the following night.

Our shortest passage to date, the one mile motor to Newlyn, was carefully planned as the easterly winds had been blowing strongly since we arrived and built up quite a sea against the harbour wall. Spirit managed to plough through the chop and we passed safely through the pier heads into the harbour which was lined with fishing vessels of all sizes. A big notice, a short way along the pontoon we tied up to, advised 'No Yachts Beyond this Point'. We were struggling to get our shore power lead to work and asked a nearby visiting sailor for advice. He helpfully pointed out where the harbourmaster was and explained that he was held up in Newlyn waiting for a new propeller to be fitted as one of the blades on his current one had fallen off! This friendly sailor's name was Colin and unbeknown to us at the time we were to cross tracks with him again further on in our voyage.

With some relief, we saw the sea had calmed down the following morning when we left early bound for Scilly. The wind was fair, about 10 to 12 knots all the way and again an easterly almost dead behind us. Whilst a lot more comfortable than beating into the wind, this point of sail has its challenges as the boat is prone to roll from side to side. It helps to have both sails out to steady this movement but it's difficult to keep them filled with wind. To ensure the main sail didn't gybe Richard rigged up a preventer, a rope holding it in place from the bow of the boat. As we cleared Land's End into open water the waves gradually increased and we had a rolling swell taking us towards the Islands. The passage of just under 40 miles took us eight hours to complete. With some excitement and not a little relief, we eventually passed through St Mary's sound, navigating the many rocks and ledges into the calm of the little harbour of the main island, where we picked up one of the visitor mooring buoys.

The Isles of Scilly are one of the Shangri-Las of sailing. Whilst not far offshore they face the full force of the Atlantic Ocean weather. Many sailors aspire to reach them yet only some succeed. They are a magical archipelago comprising 140 islands with white sandy beaches, turquoise sea and sub-tropical plants. There is little development in Scilly and, whilst popular in the holidays, we thought there would be few visitors at the end of April. We were amazed to learn that we had happened on one of the busiest weekends of the year, with St Mary hosting the World Pilot Gig Championships.

3

The Enchanted Isles of Scilly

APRIL 29TH 2022

Over the weekend of our arrival, Hugh Town in St Mary's buzzed with activity and excitement as 120 gigs were raced by their several crews in the Ladies and Mens, Veterans, Supervets and Open classes. These beautifully crafted wooden rowing boats were originally built in the 17th century to deliver pilots, the local navigators who assisted ships safely into port, under oar to the larger vessels. In 1848, 200 men were still working as pilots in Scilly using gigs. These craft also provided the means to rescue shipwreck survivors: the first account of this comes from 1666 when they went to the aid of the ship Royal Oak. Other less ethical activities are also recounted, where ships were lured to their doom on stormy nights and the gigs launched to salvage booty to boost the islanders' meagre living.

This prestigious event attracted gig clubs from all over the southwest and from further afield including Norfolk, London and Holland. The boats had been shipped in over the past several weeks, complete with their road trailers, by the passenger ship Scillonian and cargo vessel Maritha, both of which serve the islands on a daily basis.

The races, run in rounds, provided a wonderful spectacle with wave upon wave of the 12 boat groups vying against each other between the islands of St Mary's and St Agnes. The scoring was a complete mystery to us until we struck up conversation with some of the Clevedon Women's team who explained the basic rules and rowing techniques. We cheered Stella, Clare and Maria on as they raced in their yellow and blue painted gig Watch and Pray. The championships built to a crescendo during the finals, with teams and supporters cheering magnificently from the shore and quay. It was a fun and uplifting experience to be with so many people enjoying their sport and each other.

This was our third visit sailing to Scilly (the islanders prefer Scilly or The Isles of Scilly rather than The Scillies) and we found it as unspoilt as we remembered. There were encouraging signs of eco-friendliness with electric vans for islanders to hire as needed and electric golf buggies that visitors could rent, reminiscent of those in the 1967 sci-fi series The Prisoner that some of you may remember. One of the many wonderful characteristics of Scilly is the absence of visiting cars or motor vehicles.

On Bank Holiday Monday we walked along country lanes and pine-treed paths to rediscover the atmospheric prehistoric sites of Halangy Down, the Iron Age Village, built circa 800BC and Innisdgen Bronze Age Entrance Graves. We hardly passed a soul on the way or at the sites. We could almost imagine the simple yet comfortable lifestyle those ancient families were thought to have enjoyed, as we looked from their hillside vantage point over the other islands which, at that time, would have been largely joined. This small community farmed, kept their own animals and fished. They spun yarn for clothes and cast pewter as well as working iron. The land was rich in resources for the number of people that lived there and life was thought to have been peaceful. They would have looked similar to us, a strange yet captivating thought.

The Entrance Graves, also beautifully preserved, are far, far older dating between 3,000 and 4,000 years BC. They are thought to have been built and revered as shrines and places of ceremony, as well as burial sites. We also discovered Carreg Dhu, a gem of a community garden, with dense sub-tropical plants, created in a disused quarry. A few minutes' walk along the track from the gardens, Longstone café, part of an attractive farmhouse renovation, provided us with sumptuous scones and a pot of hot tea.

View from St Mary's across to Tresco

Arriving on a boat and living on board is an altogether different experience from booking into shore-based accommodation. Our whole world revolves around the safety of our ship which is not just home but the means of survival. Every day we record the atmospheric pressure and study the weather forecast to check we are secure in our current location and if not, where we can move to. On this extended trip we used a variety of sources including the Met Office marine forecasts; windfinder.com, windy. com and local coastguard VHF weather transmissions. When the wind veered round to the northwest, meaning that a swell would enter Hugh Town harbour making it uncomfortable, we decided to leave our mooring buoy and anchor in Porth Cressa on the south side of St Mary. Then, a few days later, when the wind backed to the southwest, we had to move again and chose The Cove on St Agnes. Anchoring had the added advantage of being free which helped to keep our costs down.

Away from a marina there is no easy access to the shore or to top up with water, fuel and power. Supplies are sometimes available in harbours and in Hugh Town we rafted against another boat alongside the quay to fill up with water. In the spirit of the rowed pilot gigs we paddled our tender, an inflatable dinghy, to get ashore from Spirit, rather than using our outboard.

In St Mary's, I visited the Tourist Information Centre on Porth Cressa beach. I enjoyed a warm reception from the staff who showed great concern for the seals when I explained how they were getting entangled and injured in plastic flying rings. I gave them some leaflets and they were keen to have more for the season which Hilda from FoHS kindly sent. Thankfully, I found no flying rings in the few shops that were selling beach toys. The staff were happy to chat to me and assured me that they would not be selling rings and were also looking at eco-friendly alternatives to plastic. None of the people I met had heard of the plight of the seals.

*

Talking to people in Falmouth and Scilly I realised how much we had raised awareness about the seals in Norfolk. The campaign had been launched by Peter on Winterton beach in July 2019 and, due to the excellent links the group have with the media, attracted widespread coverage from ITV Anglia and the local press: the Great Yarmouth Mercury and the Eastern Daily Press (EDP). A tremendous amount of effort had then gone into distributing our publicity along the coast from Great Yarmouth to King's Lynn. I had foot-padded the towns of Cromer, Sheringham and Wells-next-the-Sea whilst FoHS wardens covered Great Yarmouth up to Bacton. We had all talked to shops appealing to their intrinsic love of nature and in particular of seals and I found that the owner of K. Hardware in Cromer had already destroyed his stock of flying rings to protect the seals! Coastal Parish Councils came on board displaying our poster on their notice boards, Blakeney Harbour added the feature to their website for their 600 members and the seal trip boats took leaflets for their customers.

I had also heard of an independent action taken by Gorleston Beach Clean Group, near Great Yarmouth. They had seen the photos of an increasing number of seals being spotted caught in the plastic flying rings and had raised some money to buy 250 rings, the stock of a local beach shop, whose owner pledged not to sell any more. The other beach shops along Gorleston front followed suit.

Hearing of such positive actions as this was making it all worthwhile.

*

Back on board Spirit, the jobs list continued to demand attention and Richard scaled the mast to check on our rigging. This is a routine, visual inspection as part of his preventative maintenance programme. Catching potential problems early can avoid more serious issues at a later date. Climbing the mast in the Bosun's chair, he checked there were no loose fittings or chafe on the wires that hold up the mast.

The Isles of Scilly are well known for their wealth of flora and fauna, including hundreds of species of bird that stop off to rest and refuel at the Islands during their migrations. I enjoyed a nature walk in Bryher with Will Wagstaff, one of the local guides, who shared his inexhaustible love and knowledge about plants, birds, animals, geology and history of Scilly with the group. He enabled us to identify meadow and rock pipits, who dive from a height into vegetation, bandit-marked male wheatears and the cream coloured females, stonechats, the males with their striking black heads and white collar, also linnets, dunlin, ringed plover, turnstone and a migrant male great northern diver. Swallows, late in their arrival this year, were soaring and swooping over the fields and beaches catching insects. Out at sea was a gathering of razorbills and on the rocks off Hell Bay a group of grey seals, the wind carrying their eerie calls to us. Kneeling down we discovered the tiny blue-flowered dwarf pansy and a myriad of other plants, some indigenous others introduced, such as the striking purple Whistling Jack gladioli. Many mainland birds are resident and thrive in Scilly such as song thrushes, blackbirds, goldfinch, wrens, sparrows and linnets. What is striking is their lack of fear since there are few predators and they seem to regard humans as relatively safe.

Seeing and hearing the seals reminded me of my one experience of seeing a seal underwater. I was snorkelling off the Eastern Isles in Scilly on a previous trip, just floating and looking down, when a little head popped out of the thick bed of kelp: it was a young seal! It looked straight up at me then disappeared back into its hidey hole, wary I'm sure of the large non-seal shape suspended above. It struck me how absolutely at home the seal was living under the waves and amongst the seaweed. Seals haul out to rest, digest their food, moult and breed. Their movement is quite cumbersome on land and they are wary of being disturbed which causes them to lose vital energy reserves. In the sea they transform into sleek, agile mammals with a lightening quickness and an endearing curiosity.

*

Seals are one of our most iconic sea mammals. Two species are native to Britain, Atlantic grey seals and harbour or common seals.

Grey seals are nearly twice the size of a harbour seal with a male (bull) seal weighing up to 300kg, that is 47 stone! All seals are adapted to hold their breath under water and do this for an average of 10 to 16 minutes though they can stay under for twice as long.

Harbour seals generally dive to a depth of around 50 metres and greys 70 metres though a grey seal is capable of diving far deeper: up to 300 metres. It is little known that the grey seal is rare globally. About 40% of the world's population live around the coast of the British Isles and are most numerous in Scottish waters. Grey seals are only found in the North Atlantic as far east as the Baltic and the North Sea.

Seals regularly haul out to rest, digest their food, groom, recover from deep dives, and sleep at favoured remote spots on our coasts. They also spend time ashore to give birth to their pups and to moult, shedding worn fur and growing a new coat that protects them from the cold of the sea and streamlines them as they swim and hunt for fishy prey.

Both species are with us all year and both widely disperse for long periods when they will be less visible. They are able to nap at sea and are known to take long journeys: swimming along the coasts and crossing over to Europe. Yet many people are unaware of this and have never seen a seal in the wild.

Harbour seals give birth in the summer, greys in the winter. Whilst harbour seal pups can swim a few hours after birth, greys are born clothed in a soft, white fur coat which is not properly waterproof. Grey seals return to traditional 'rookery' sites to give birth and mate. Newborn grey seals pups suckle for about three weeks. After that the mother/pup bond ends and the mother mates and leaves her pup. Ideally by this time the pup will have stored supplies of fat from their mother's very rich milk and should weigh 40-45 kilos. The stored fat will provide all the nourishment the pup needs for a further period of up to three weeks while it moults its baby fur and grows its properly waterproof coat. Only then is it ready to start life at sea, doing this instinctively, learning how to swim and catch food. Mortality is very high, around 40% of pups do not complete the first year of life.

During their first six weeks grey seal pups are extremely vulnerable. They spend most of the time sleeping ashore with little movement in order to conserve their energy. Their main threats are from human disturbance, dog attacks and stormy weather when high tides can sweep them off the beach. A mother may leave her pup for a few hours but she will keep an eye on it, if her line of sight is broken by people surrounding her pup she may abandon it and the pup will starve to death. Pups have also drowned because people have, in their ignorance, encouraged them into the sea when they cannot swim properly or they are tired.

*

We had reached our last day in Scilly. The winds were forecast to increase the following week and we had a long passage ahead off the exposed north Cornish coast. We wanted to reach Padstow whilst the weather was calm and fair. Passage planning is pivotal to our life onboard, this takes account of distances to be covered, wind and tide direction, if there is enough tidal height to leave and arrive and weather, weather, weather, whether to go! All these things dictate our movements, where we go and how long we can stay.

On that final morning I sat on deck with a morning cuppa enjoying complete peace and calm, bathed in the song of shore birds and gulls. A razorbill came and fished near the boat, I could see it through the clear green blue water as it dived. I then donned my wetsuit and realised my wish to swim in these beautiful waters. With my mask on I could see our anchor was well buried then Richard paddled me ashore to snorkel above gently waving sea weed, rocks covered in limpets and a shoal of little sand eels, perfect!

Back on board I was trying to peel my wetsuit off sitting in the cockpit. I bought this suit many years ago and I must have put on a bit of weight as it was so tight I could not wear a costume underneath and I was having difficulty extricating myself. Just as I had managed to peel off the top half we heard a cheery, 'Hello' from the couple in the nearby boat who were waving as they passed alongside in their dinghy!

The infamous wetsuit!

4

Doom Bar and
Crossing The Bristol Channel

MAY 8TH 2022

We awoke at dawn on May 8th to find mist in the bay. Ahead of us lay the 70-mile passage to Padstow. Predictions had warned of the possibility of fog patches at first clearing later, but with our radar on we could see other boats on the screen so, whilst taking great care, we motored in fog from Scilly towards Land's End. There is a traffic separation scheme (TSS) off Land's End. Similar to a virtual motorway, it regulates ships which must stay in the correct lane. Other smaller vessels like ours have to cross the lanes at right angles to cover the scheme over the shortest possible distance. It's a bit like being a hedgehog crossing the road. A ship-free zone midway provides safety and we used this to regain our northerly course before crossing the far side. Thankfully, we came out of the bank of fog before entering the TSS and had clear views of the ships. We also had a good sighting of a grey seal a little way off our port side. The seal was resting in a vertical position called bottling with his or her head lifted to the heavens, a beautiful sight.

The north Cornish coast lived up to its exposed reputation. Whilst the winds started fair and we hoisted full sails, as we neared Newquay a gusty blow suddenly filled in from the southeast. We reefed the sails accordingly and

A seal bottling

later found other boats too had been taken by surprise. It would take us 12 or 13 hours to reach Padstow and we had decided to anchor in a recommended cove nearby and enter the following morning. This was to avoid navigating the infamous Doom Bar at night, a drying sand bank across the entrance to the Camel estuary, which has a fearsome reputation for kicking up a nasty sea. We found Mother Ivey's Bay, chose a spot nestled in between rocks and dropped our anchor. I was a bit anxious about the anchor holding secure overnight and when I woke in the dark, I checked to make sure we had not moved. Richard slept soundly, no worries there!

Padstow Harbour is reminiscent of Penzance, a traditional dock with lock gates that were installed after the town was severely flooded in the 1980s. The approach to the harbour dries at low water so we had to time our entry.

This we did, but when we arrived we found the lock gates closed! After a quick reassessment and directions from the harbourmaster we rafted up against a French boat which had also sailed from Scilly. The gates were then opened for a very short time at the top of the tide and we all proceeded into the inner harbour to take up our allocated berths. Cosy and still, we slept well that night.

Padstow is an attractive old town with streets tumbling down to the harbour lined with cottages, no doubt inhabited in past years by fishing folk. Now it is a very popular resort with holiday cottages, chic shops and of course Rick Stein's famous seafood restaurant – too pricey for us though we did try his fish, halloumi burger and chips take-away. We were right in the middle of the action. Climbing the harbour ladder we surfaced next to the ice cream van with a pub opposite and people enjoying their cones. Back in our cockpit we overheard one mum explaining to her little girl, 'Yes that's a man sitting on his boat, eating a sandwich' – we were evidently part of the harbour scene!

On our first morning after arriving I was able to turn the immersion heater on, something we can only use when plugged into shore power. Sometime later, I heard a yelp from Richard. He had got used to hand showering his private parts in cold water in the Scillies whilst we were at anchor and had not realised the immersion was on!

As we were trying to avoid marinas as much as possible, we had to be self-sufficient and prepared to rough it in commercial harbours and docks. Part of this process required the use of a fender board, a long plank which spans across the wooden posts on quay walls and prevented our fenders dropping into the gap between them, which would potentially damage our boat. This came into good use in Padstow. We also had the chance to water up again and top up our batteries on shore power.

Looking around Padstow, I found the three shops selling beach toys all stocked flying rings, so I went into seal campaign mode to talk to the staff and raise awareness of the dangers of the rings to seals. I always aim to be courteous in my approach and try to get a conversation going, but on these occasions the staff were quite defensive, perhaps because they had been unaware of the problem or didn't know what they could do.

The assistants at the Tourist Information Centre and Sealife Safaris were, in contrast, helpful and positive and I also sent an e-mail to Rick Stein asking him to support the petition to ban flying rings. Once again, none of the people I had talked to were aware that flying rings were posing a danger to seals.

*

We re-launched the flying rings campaign each year and I remembered visiting Great Yarmouth in May 2021, the third year of the campaign, with an ITV Anglia camera man to film me talking to a shop owner to explain the dangers of flying rings to seals. I arrived early to test the ground and see if any of the shop keepers would talk to me. I entered the first shop selling beach toys and as soon as I started to explain to the owner what I was doing he said, 'Oh we don't sell flying rings anymore because of the seals'! This was repeated in Regent Toy shop and all the

*others on the street. It was a heartening response and an accolade
to the local shop keepers and Councillors who had been spreading
the word.*

*

Relaxing back on Spirit we were looking at who was
moored in the harbour when we recognised the boat in
front of us: it was Bella Vela, Colin's boat with the broken
propeller, who we had met in Newlyn. It was great to meet
up again and he recounted his experiences of having a new
propeller cast and fitted by the local engineering shop in
Newlyn.

We had thought we would be in Padstow for most of the
week, but the weather dictated we needed to leave after
only a couple of nights. This was slightly tricky as our next
journey north to Milford Haven was another long one,
which we wanted to achieve in daylight, but the lock gates
of the harbour only opened at 2pm. The harbourmaster
sorted this out by ringing the RNLI to ask if we could make
use of their mooring buoy (which was out in the estuary)
for the night, a regular occurrence here, so we could leave
at dawn the following day.

Planning this next leg had taken time and discussion. We
had wanted to visit Lundy to experience the island and
see some of the wildlife there, but when we checked the
almanac, the sailors' bible, it showed strong tides and
'races', areas of unsettled water, around the island. We
needed two days of settled, calm weather but there were
strong winds forecast to arrive soon so we reluctantly
decided the safest course was to make straight for Milford
Haven on the one-day favourable window we had.

During the night before leaving for a long passage I'm often a bit anxious, the chatter in my mind raises all sorts of unsettling what ifs. On this occasion, strong winds had come and gone but I woke up wondering what sort of swell they had left and what might be coming in from the Atlantic. Getting up and getting on with it usually helps and we both rose soon after 4am, ready to leave at 5am. There was quite a chop getting out of the estuary over Doom Bar, then as we cleared land, on practically a northerly course, we settled into a steadier rhythm with a fair westerly wind on the beam. There was quite a swell but no breaking waves and we fairly romped most of the way. This makes it sound a short passage, it definitely was not and I helmed for several hours, the best way I have found to keep a settled tummy, before collapsing below for a long nap whilst Richard kept watch.

We were sailing in tandem with Colin on Bella Vela. En route, we tracked a coaster ship that came quite close to us but passed in front. Colin was ahead and we were glad to hear the ship sound a single blast, indicating it was turning to starboard to avoid him. About halfway across the Bristol Channel we saw land to our right in the distance, it was the Island of Lundy and as we were passing I heard a slight splash. A pod of dolphins had joined us, the first we had seen on this voyage. They came in twos and threes here and there swimming alongside, in front, under and behind Spirit. It is just a lovely, uplifting experience every time we see them and it made us miss visiting Lundy even more. Nearer to Wales, we spotted our first puffins! Alongside the guillemots we could distinguish them by their shorter, stubbier form, colours and flight. They kept flying past in both directions to and from land, in pairs and sometimes threes or fours, probably coming out to sea to fish and returning to their nesting islands of Skomer and Skokholm.

After negotiating a tanker that was exiting Milford Haven entrance, we found our way to the picturesque anchorage at Dale. In the distance behind Milford Haven were the industrial towers, leviathan ships and lights of the oil terminals, looking just like the gates of Mordor in Tolkien's epic tale 'The Lord of the Rings'. We laid out 40 metres of chain and our 10 metre snubber, a length of stretchy line rigged to stop the chain snatching, to hold us in the strong winds forecast. We were preparing some food, when we noticed Colin had arrived and anchored not far away. We were glad he had made it in before dark and continued with our tea. A little while later, before turning in, we looked out again and thought that Bella Vela had moved. We kept watching and sure enough Colin's boat was dragging its anchor – it was almost on top of a buoy that had been a good way off when he had arrived. It was now getting dark and there was little we could do, his radio was turned off and we had no mobile number to contact him. Thankfully, he appeared on deck, raised his anchor and moved to a better spot where he found good holding.

We learnt some years ago that it is the sailor's prerogative to sleep and eat whenever possible! Truly, because when you are on passage you need all the energy you can muster and on arrival in port or a safe anchorage, you need to catch up on your reserves. Accordingly, on Friday morning there was no call to rise, we slept and slept with a clear conscience. We were keen though, to explore the tiny hamlet of Dale, where amazingly Henry VII landed his men in 1485 before marching against Richard III at the

Battle of Bosworth and, of more immediate importance, to find the Boathouse café. We rang to check on opening times and found to our horror we only had half an hour to get there. We pumped up our dinghy, fitted the outboard and threw in oars and rucksacks in a record time of 20 minutes. We made the café! That evening, we picked up Colin from his yacht and enjoyed a few drinks in the local pub exchanging some hilarious seafaring adventures and boat maintenance tips.

Again, the weather determined our next move. There were more strong winds forecast, this time from the east-southeast, which would make Dale Bay untenable as there is a long fetch from this direction and waves would build up into the anchorage. We decided to head upriver and set off motoring across to the port of Milford Haven dodging past vast oil tankers and their manoeuvring tugs. Carried by the flooding tide we ducked under Cleddau Bridge following the deep water channel as the river twisted and turned. The scenery changed from an industrial landscape to wooded shores with overhanging trees as we sought the refuge of a sheltered and secure mooring at Lawrenny Yacht Station.

5

Milford Haven –
a Relaxing, Wet Interlude

MAY 14TH, 2022

The moorings at Lawrenny Yacht Station lay just off the main river to starboard on the river Carew. They were listed in the nautical almanac at £5 per night, which seemed too good to be true, and bookable in advance, but we had not been able to get a reply to our phone calls. We arrived late in the afternoon at the top of the tide and luckily, we thought at the time, a river patrol boat happened to be nearby. Seeking their advice about which buoy to pick up, they pointed to the first one at the mouth of the river. We tied on and ate our evening meal. We were not inclined to dinghy ashore as the ebb tide was starting to run fast down the river and into the main channel, stronger than the flood with the additional force and volume of the river water, and we were a fair distance from the landing place. Feeling secure, away from the open anchorage at Dale, we enjoyed another good night's sleep.

The next morning, Sunday, we doubted we would find the Yacht Station's office in the chandlery open and almost went straight to an inviting looking café above the quay. We thought we would just try the door anyway and it opened. The friendly owner apologised and said she had been trying to ring us. She wondered if we would be happy to move buoys as the one we were on had been 'condemned by the divers'. She said not to worry it was probably just a loose shackle (!) but it might be an idea to move anyway, which we heartily agreed with. Our bill for five nights came to £105, a normal price for mooring buoys and yes, our expectation had been too good to be true. We did visit the café, which had Wi-Fi, and walked to the village of Lawrenny to give the strong tide time to ease before moving to our new, safer buoy conveniently close to the landing pontoon.

We found ourselves in a quiet, scenic spot at Lawrenny with ancient oak-wooded riversides filled with birdsong and an occasional house or cottage half hidden by the trees. The area sits within the Pembrokeshire National Park. Swallows and house martins skimmed and swooped above the river and a heron flew low past the boat one evening. Large grey, silvered mullet sheltered under the dinghy when we tied it up on the old wooden quay.

There was an impressive high quay wall and when we talked to the owner's son we were amazed to hear that large sailing ships once stopped here to offload their ballast boulders, before taking on cargo, onto what is now a gently sloping lawn dotted with daisies, buttercup and wooden chalets. This came to be known as Ballast Hill. One of the main cargoes to be collected was coal. Also, during WW2, from 1941 to 1943, Lawrenny Quay was a sea-plane training station for patrol bomber pilots flying Sunderland Flying Boats. We had noticed an outsized landing slip built, we now discovered, to bring the planes ashore, we had not realised its significance.

When we dug a bit deeper into the history of this area we discovered that around 1700 BC the famous 80 Bluestones destined for Stonehenge were moved from the Prescelly Mountains, where they had been quarried, down river to Milford Haven on their journey towards Dorset. A number of cromlechs, Megalithic tombs, dotted around attest to an earlier civilisation. In later centuries smuggling was rife, with hideouts in the tributaries and creeks such as the river Carew.

The Yacht Station seemed hardly to have changed over the past 50 years. Behind the chalets were some static caravans hidden amongst the trees. A concrete shower block stood in the middle of them. Armed with 50p pieces we both braved the cold and basic facilities, with 'Psycho' type plastic shower curtains and no hairdryer. Two times 50p was meant to last for 6 minutes, sufficient time for a hair wash and shower surely? I washed my hair and then got lathered up only for the shower to cease! I found out afterwards that Richard had the same experience, but he had all the change so was able to keep feeding the meter. I thought briefly about running round to Richard's side wrapped in a towel to collect more 50ps, then decided instead to just rinse off in the hand basin within the communal wash area. Sadly, I found the hot water tap there ran cold. I left an embarrassingly large pool of water on the floor.

Lawrenny village is really a hamlet where only a hundred souls live. There is a post box, St Caradoc's church and the community shop, a very rare amenity whose advantages we enjoyed when we visited at the highly selective opening time on Monday between 3 and 4pm. We were welcomed by the two volunteers on duty, and two barking black and white spaniels, one of whom tried to shake my hand with his mouth! The volunteers explained that the opening hours were just for visitors as all the residents have a fob and can help themselves, settling up their accounts later. The church dates back to the 12th century, has an enormous tower and the broken prone statue of a mysterious unknown knight which we reckoned was a Knight Templar as legend associates King Arthur with this area.

We were very glad to have found refuge in Lawrenny, as the winds did blow hard from the east, then south and it poured with rain on and off for much of the week. Although the rain was much needed as the spring had been dry here, it was not much fun to be sailing in it. We did enjoy the pub for toasties, fish and chips and the amazingly efficient Wi-Fi which allowed us to download several films at a rate of knots. We were becoming frighteningly dependent on being linked into the internet, so much so that Richard refused a pretty, three-mile walk above the rivers through gnarled oaks choosing instead to do his 'maintenance research' in the pub!

Whilst in Lawrenny, I was pleased to receive a reply from Rick Stein's personal assistant saying:

'Thank you for your email regarding the plight of our seals from the flying rings that they get caught up in, it's absolutely tragic....we have put the information on our internal communications platform for all of our (700-plus) staff to see and hope they will be touched by this and sign up to the petition...Thank you for bringing this to our attention.'

It was gratifying to receive a personal reply so promptly and heartening that Rick's PA showed concern and had taken action to help.

We extended our stay at Lawrenny to take us to a week, at a welcome discounted price, and took a walk alongside the River Cresswell through fields and woods to the very attractive quay of the same name and the Cresselly Arms. This old, traditional pub served only drinks and displayed a notice at the door 'Strictly no children or dogs'! It was like stepping back in time. We sipped drinks in the cool, dark interior then sat on the quayside munching our pack-ups and watching swallows flitting down to collect mud from the river bank to build their nests and mallard ducks chaperoning their ducklings.

We planned to leave Lawrenny the following day and return to the anchorage at Dale as the wind had changed from east to west offering shelter again. The forecast over the following days was still a bit mixed but we planned to make our way around to St David's Head and thence cross to Ireland, hoping to see more puffins en route.

6

Flat Batteries, a Rescue and Ireland!

MAY 21ST, 2022

Before leaving Lawrenny we did a nifty ferry glide, moving the yacht sideways using the tide, across to the landing pontoon to water up. We then motored back down the river to Dale Bay giving the Rosslare Irish ferry a wide berth. We planned to visit Skomer Island, in search of puffins, then return to Dale as strong winds were again forecast for the rest of the week. We picked up a mooring buoy to tuck in close inshore.

In the early hours we were woken by a sound, 'beep beep… beep beep'. Richard investigated and found it was the low voltage alarm on the domestic batteries; we had lost a lot of charge. He turned off the alarm and went back to sleep, we would deal with it in the morning. The planned trip to Skomer was not to be.

Sunday morning was spent trouble shooting. Out came the multimeter again, 'to measure is to know'. The battery monitor was saying we still had 78% of charge available but a quick test with the meter across the actual battery terminals confirmed they were both dead, well dead. It didn't take long to figure out that the battery monitor had been misleading us, it had got out of sync with its capacity algorithm. To put it more simply, we had been unknowingly running the batteries down to almost zero charge since we left Portsmouth, when they should never be taken below 50%. As they were renewed in September this was more than a little frustrating!

The nearest chandlery in Neyland, just up from the town of Milford Haven, was closed on Sunday but first thing Monday morning a quick phone call secured two replacement batteries of the correct size ready for us to collect later in the day, phew, what a relief! We motored back up the Haven to Neyland, which is on the port side just before Cleddau Bridge, on the flood tide watching out for a huge tanker being escorted into dock by three tugs. A narrow but well-buoyed channel brought us straight into an easy berth. We went straight to the chandlery to fetch our new batteries then treated ourselves in the marina café to all-day breakfasts.

In the end our visit to Neyland Marina was a welcome break. We had the rest of the day to catch up with boat care: fitting the batteries, scrubbing the decks, washing our faithful dinghy, taking a fuel sample from the bottom of the tank to check for impurities, and the next morning making use of the marina's laundry and provisioning up at the local Co-op.

In a nearby berth we noticed an E-Boat. This is a very small 22-foot sailing yacht which was our first boat after progressing from dinghies. We regularly trailered our E-Boat Eider from our home in Yorkshire to Pwhelli, North Wales before getting fed up with this and keeping her there on a permanent berth. We had various adventures, trials and tribulations in Eider until we finally realised we needed a boat that was bigger and a bit more stable and seaworthy.

That evening, I managed to fit in a walk along Westfield Pill, the small inlet we were on where, amazingly, ships were built from the 1760s for almost a century. The land had then been bought by the South Wales Railway and a terminus built. Brunel, the Victorian engineer, oversaw this development and the area prospered from being a railway hub and ferry port until 1906. The disused railway is now Brunel's Trail, a cycle track running for 14 miles, and Westfield Pill is a nature reserve. Steep wooded banks rise up from the inlet and trail providing a safe wildlife habitat for an array of species and two small lakes offer a safe haven for water and sea birds in poor weather. I had put on rain gear and sure enough there was a complete downpour as I returned, I still got pretty wet!

Later that evening we found the cheapest, cash only, takeaways so far on our trip in Neyland town. Richard's fish and chips cost him a mere £5.60 with an extra £1 for baked beans and I had a handsome portion of Chinese mixed vegetable noodles in satay sauce for £5.30. What a result, both meals were delicious.

Motoring back down the river to Dale Bay on Tuesday I picked up a message from David at Friends of Horsey Seals. A media company had contacted him, saying they were looking into a feature on seals getting caught in plastic flying rings and could they talk to me about the campaign and our sailing trip. This was a total surprise and a fantastic opportunity, so I immediately returned their call and we discussed what was needed for the feature and how I could help.

Consequently, after securing Spirit back in Dale at the anchorage with 40 metres of chain in preparation for the strong westerly winds forecast, we spent part of the following day taking some short video clips. These involved showing me in action arriving in our dinghy onto the landing pontoon at Dale (several takes being required to catch me lassoing the cleat first time) and interviewing Tony who runs the tiny beach shop at the café about the campaign. Tony kindly agreed to be videoed by Richard whilst we talked about the dangers posed to seals by plastic flying rings. He had not heard of the problem and when I explained he was shocked and concerned. He promised to pass the message on.

Talking about the campaign with Tony in Dale village

*

Feeling so passionately that seals need to be kept safe from flying rings has enabled me to stretch my comfort zone in ways I could never have imagined before the campaign. Appearing on TV is a good example. At the start of 2020 I spent the weekend before the Covid lockdown helping two friends, one of them a sculptor, make Sealy, a life size model of an adult grey seal with a flying ring embedded around its neck. Made of eco-friendly plaster of paris and painted with mottled spots of browns and black, it really did look lifelike. ITV responded to a press release and Sealy and I were interviewed in my garden explaining about the campaign and the disastrous effects of plastic flying rings on seals when they get caught in them.

When restrictions eased, I took Sealy on a beach tour, supported by volunteers, Richard and friends, to coastal towns and beaches providing a stunning, self-explanatory display of the danger of flying rings. The vast majority of visitors, families and children we spoke to were shocked when they saw the display and photos of the seals entangled in flying rings. They were deeply concerned about the unnecessary suffering caused by people losing and discarding the rings and wanted to help the seals. One woman had just bought a flying ring for her young son to play with on the beach, she said she had no idea of the harm it could cause seals and gave it to us to destroy.

Sealy the life size sculpture

Seeing the problem with the rings, many people then made the link to the general problem of plastic waste getting into the sea and harming marine wildlife.

Entanglement in fishing nets and line is another huge hazard for seals and other sea animals and birds. The reason I had focused on flying rings was that this was an unnecessary danger that could be tackled with everyone's help. As awareness grew people were saying to us, 'flying rings shouldn't be sold as beach toys' and 'people shouldn't be throwing them on the beach'.

*

For the next two days the wind blew hard from the west. We decided to venture ashore in the dinghy on Wednesday as Thursday was showing a further increase in wind strength which might have made the trip risky. On Spirit the water was relatively calm but once in our tender we could feel the little waves much more and had to motor quite fast to try and ride over them. Although we had our full waterproofs on, we took an absolute soaking with spray coming over the front of the dinghy as we headed into the shore, about quarter of a mile away. This confirmed our decision not to repeat the trip next day, so were confined to the ship.

The weather fronts were due to pass through with fair weather setting in from Friday morning. We consequently made our second plan to set off for Skomer early to catch the last of the fair tide and I set the alarm for 4am. During the night I woke to hear the wind still howling, it continued through to dawn. It takes time, perhaps two tides, for the sea to calm after strong winds, so I decided to postpone our departure at least until the afternoon, and we went back to a welcome sleep. Friday was a lovely day and at last we set off, catching the later tide, to the fabled island of Skomer, breeding site for thousands of puffins also guillemots, razorbills, Manx shearwaters and many other species.

Protected marine reserves such as Lundy and Skomer are not easy to access, a good thing as it helps protect their wildlife. To get to Skomer you can brave Jack Sound which is one of the top 11 notorious tidal races in Britain along with Portland Bill, or go round the outside making sure you avoid Wild Goose Race off the island. This was our choice, although it was twice the distance. Whilst the waves had calmed, they were strange and eerie as we approached the island and we could see and feel the strong currents underneath the surface. It was only as we came close to the rocky shores that we began to make out the birds flying and circling. Tiny specks at first, they grew into the unmistakable forms of puffins with their bright orange feet and beautifully marked bills and heads, guillemots with dark grey backs, and razorbills jet black with a white streak on their broad bills. There are four visitor mooring buoys in North Haven at Skomer and as we approached the tiny rocky bay, we saw that there were boats already in. Luckily, the last buoy was free and we gratefully picked it up.

Whilst we were too late to land on the island, we enjoyed an amazing spectacle all evening of mixed rafts of birds resting and preening in the water all around us. Puffins popped in and out of their burrows on the steep slopes above, courting and occasionally arguing with an interloper. Guillemots collected together in their rocky colony and razorbills were scattered all over, nesting on rocks and at burrow entrances. More and more puffins arrived, numbers have thankfully increased and over 38,000 were counted here in April, until the sky above us was full of returning birds. Another spectacle at Skomer is the thousands of Manx shearwaters returning at night to their burrows to escape predators. We stayed up until dark then Richard retired and I persisted to 11pm, giving up regretfully as we had an early start for our passage across to Ireland. During the night I woke and I'm sure I heard the sound of the elusive shearwaters.

Rising soon after dawn, we planned to leave by 6am to catch the north-going tide to clear the islands and rocks off St David's head, then head west across the Irish sea towards Arklow. I was taking the cover off the tiller when I saw the dark form of a bird in the cockpit corner, oh no! it looked like a guillemot, and I feared it was dead. I picked up the bird gently and it came to life trying to peck me. It was a Manx shearwater. I had been reading that shearwaters can become disorientated on their return to land and look for somewhere safe to sleep, being nocturnal. But what were we to do with the bird? It was sleepy, our dinghy was deflated and tied up on board and we had a tide to catch. I'd previously made a note of the Skomer warden's phone number and rang it just hoping there would be an answer, despite it being 5.50am. There was, thank goodness, and half an hour later Leighton Newman, previously warden at Blakeney in Norfolk, boarded Spirit and deftly transferred the beautiful Manx shearwater into a safe holding-bag. He said he had a nesting box for it to rest in before release. What a complete relief.

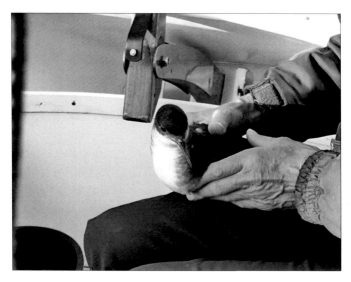

Rescuing the Manx shearwater

I was on cloud nine for the rest of the day after our rescue and from having seen so many puffins up close in their natural habitat. Not quite so much Richard who was mortified by the guano splatters all over the boat! It looked like someone had been using Spirit for paintball target practice, he complained.

We had a good passage across the Irish Sea that Saturday May 28th with sunny, clear blue skies, mainly calm seas and north-northeasterly winds which were not ideal, but we managed to keep our sails up for most of the trip, using our engine to keep up speed when the tide turned foul. We reached Arklow by 7.30pm, rafted up against a friendly French boat and walked into the little town to enjoy a late Chinese meal. We had made it to Ireland!

Earlier, when we were settling Spirit onto the visitor pontoon, a friendly local boat owner came along and asked if we were OK and had everything we needed. We were having problems getting the shore power to work and he explained that the unit on the pontoon was tripping for some reason and that he would let the harbour chap know. He also cautioned us to 'wash your hands if any of your lines get wet as the river is polluted with raw sewage'! We had noticed the river Avoca looked brown and had an unfortunate odour, but never imagined this could be the cause.

The next morning we met the 'chap' who turned out to be the owner of the marina. He confirmed that the town's raw sewage gets pumped into the river but there are plans to build a new treatment facility to prevent this, which should be ready in three years' time. When we asked 'What about the poor fish and wildlife in the meanwhile?' he replied we shouldn't worry about the fish because the copper leaching from the disused copper mine further up the river had killed them all anyway. With a smile he added 'That's one of the advantages of keeping a boat in Arklow, nothing grows on the hull!' We researched the river Avoca and found it is indeed one of the nine most polluted rivers in Ireland.

We raised the issue of the faulty power unit on the pontoon and the marina owner helpfully produced another three way adaptor to plug into the already overloaded domestic extension lead. We prayed it didn't rain. When we proffered payment he replied it was cash only, payable to him and not to worry about it now, as he would be down later after he had been home to cut his grass. It was gradually dawning on us that this was rather a unique marina! We withdrew the cash required – not expensive at only 50 Euros for two nights.

Sharing the pontoon with other visiting boats and crew we chatted and swapped information with some of them. The following morning the couple from Zephyr, the yacht moored behind us, asked if we had seen anyone in or near their boat the previous evening, because when they had awoken there were footprints and blood in their cockpit. We had not, though strangely we had fitted and locked our hatch washboards the previous evening for safety, which we very rarely do. Normally there is good security at marinas in the form of gates opened by codes or fobs, not so at Arklow. Perhaps some poor soul had been attacked and was hiding out on Zephyr, we will never know.

The state of the river rather spoilt our stay in Arklow and we made plans to move on after a day of recuperation. We decided to see if we could spend the night in Wicklow Harbour just 15 miles up the coast. Light westerly winds, a calm sea and fair tide provided ideal conditions for a pleasant sail up the coast. En route we made a number of attempts to call Wicklow harbourmaster for permission to enter the Harbour to no avail. We had just given up as the tide was about to sweep us past the entrance and he called us back and welcomed us in!

Here, as in Padstow, we tied up against the harbour wall, the difference being that with no lock gates the water level would rise and fall with the tide. We needed to ensure our lines were long enough not to strain against the boat when the water fell. A steep climb up a sturdy ladder gave us access to the pier.

On arriving in a port or marina the etiquette is to book in, unless turning up very late. Hence, we set off to find the harbourmaster. We walked along the river lined with fishing boats, into the little town and over a bridge into the port area, eventually finding the harbour supervisor on his own in a tiny portakabin. He was extremely helpful and declined any offer of payment for our berth insisting that the season had not started and anyway they had no facility to take a card payment, suggesting instead we make a donation to the RNLI. He furnished us with useful information about the town of Wicklow and when I asked about how we might visit Glendalough, an ancient monastic site in the Wicklow mountains, he gave a wonderful account of the various possibilities prefaced by, 'If it's Glendalough you're wanting to visit this is not the best place to be going from!' The details he furnished about public transport from Dublin to the site turned out to be spot on.

Wicklow was, in fact, a gem of a pocket sized town where we discovered an unexpectedly chic coffee shop, abbey ruins set in wildlife friendly grounds, a clean river and Bridge Street Bookshop which had won the, 'Best Bookshop in Ireland' award in 2012. In this literary treasure trove I asked the very knowledgeable and helpful owner for advice about which novel to choose by an Irish author. The descriptions of plot and setting she described were sounding a bit grim, so I asked if there was anything a bit more uplifting? She answered gaily, 'Happy, uplifting and Irish literature don't really go together!' I followed her recommendation of 'The Heart's Invisible Furies' by John Boyne, an epic tale about a gay lad growing up in Ireland.

The following day we left for the short, we thought, passage to Dun Laoghaire, in Dublin Bay. The morning was calm and sunny and the forecast was for little wind. Five miles north however, we saw a line of white tops to the waves, a sign of unsettled water. The wind was increasing significantly from the north west so we were then in a 'wind against tide' situation, which means the direction of the wind was opposing the flow of the tide, resulting in increasing, short, steep waves. The going became very tough and wet with Spirit making slow headway against the steep chop. We considered our options and decided to put into the marina at Greystones which was only three miles away. Thankfully, as we came abeam of Greystones the wind and waves started to calm and I reckoned we still had time to make Dun Laoghaire before the tide turned, which we did, taking an hour longer than planned.

Turning into the huge outer harbour of Dun Laoghaire and then into the marina could not have been of greater contrast to arriving in Arklow! It was big, protected and clean with a full range of facilities. The gates were opened with fingerprint scanning security for heaven's sake! and the town, to us, resembled Monte Carlo with its wide, open, tree-lined streets, a range of cafés and restaurants and the plush Marine Hotel and Royal Irish Yacht Club. We collapsed into a café for pick-me-up hot drinks and toasties then returned to Spirit to snooze.

With some trepidation I set off the next morning on my own pilgrimage to Glendalough in the Wicklow Mountains National Park. The journey involved taking the Dublin Bay DART (Dublin Area Rapid Transport) train, walking through the town of Barry and looking for the 181 St

Kevin's bus service at the Old Town Hall, aka McDonalds, which should take me up to the Wicklow Mountains and the ancient site at 12.10pm. I asked three people in Barry about this special bus. The first, a bus driver himself, had never heard of it; the second, a local woman, gave me clear directions to the Town Hall; and the third, an estate agent, said he had not seen it that morning and would let me know if he could find out when it was due. I waited an hour then, sure enough, St Kevin's service swept in right on time, just like the Knight Bus that plucks up Harry Potter in J.K. Rowling's famous story.

St Kevin walked to Glendalough, 'valley of the two lakes', and settled there in the 6th Century to follow a life of seclusion and contemplation. Stories abound about his extraordinary, spiritual connection with the natural world:

> 'Kevin feels the warm eggs, the small breast, the tucked Neat head and claws and, finding himself linked into the network of eternal life, is moved to pity:…'
>
> (From 'St Kevin and the Blackbird',
> poem by Seamus Heaney)

Others joined St Kevin and the community founded a monastic settlement. It is an entrancing place: the beautifully renovated Round Tower rising above church ruins, gravestones all around where once there would have been dwellings and fields for crops and animals. Steep oak-wooded hillsides rise from the lakes with views of the mountain pass beyond. The site is very popular but I found moments of quiet at the location of St Kevin's Cell and Reefert Church deep in the woods away from the main site. Birds sang all around and a cuckoo called across the valley.

Richard remained on Spirit to undertake an essential rewiring job: installing a new 240v socket for the battery charger. I hoped I would not find him burnt to a crisp on my return! All was fine and another job completed.

We had two fun days exploring the fair city of Dublin although sadly friends who were due to join us were unable to make it due to catching Covid. What to do when there is so much to choose from? We plumped for a delicious brunch at Bewley's Café; the portraits room at the Irish National Gallery; sitting with (the sculpture of) Oscar Wilde in Merrion Square Park; and the alluring exhibition about the life and works of the poet Seamus Heaney at the Irish National Bank's Cultural and Heritage Centre. In the Temple Bar quarter we lunched at Gogarty's pub whilst listening to live traditional Irish music played on the fiddle and guitar. Nearly every pub there had live music creating a friendly, entertaining atmosphere, something many towns at home, we thought, could benefit from. The excellent DART train service makes it easy to access the city from Dun Laoghaire with the station being a stone's throw from the marina.

The week had been one of extremes and contrasts, between the 'pong' of Arklow and glitz of Dun Laoghaire; the tough sail between Wicklow and Dublin Bay; and the peace of Glendalough and bustle of the city. We had been getting strong wind warnings from the local met office so we decided to pay for an extra two nights stay in Dun Laoghaire and were over the moon to be given these for free, as this would take us to a week's deal.

7

The 200 Euro Weather Forecast and Hello Scotland!

JUNE 6TH, 2022

Our final day in Dun Laoghaire Marina dawned beautiful and sunny with hardly any wind, perfect for trying the seal campaign cruising chute. We had been pouring over when to deploy this huge, light weight sail emblazoned with the seal campaign logo. They can be a real handful to fly and consequently are often left in a locker and forgotten. We had also been racking our brains as to how to get publicity pictures of the sail in action.

We rigged the system of lines required and decided to try it first with Spirit secure on her berth as the wind was so light. The sail is hoisted within a snuffer, a long sock which contains it; the snuffer is then hauled up releasing the sail and pulled down when it needs to be doused. We managed to do this and the chute filled, displaying its shocking-pink hue and seal logo. It evidently drew attention, as the skipper of a neighbouring boat came over to have a look. We admitted that we were apprehensive about sailing with the chute and he gave us not only welcome advice but the offer of leading us on his boat and coming aboard ours if we needed any help. He advised the day was perfect and he would be sailing his own boat out into Dublin bay in 10 minutes! We prevaricated for a few seconds then gratefully accepted, this was too good an opportunity to miss and Fia, the skipper, was also happy to take pictures of the sail for us.

It all went according to plan; we managed to control the sail and wafted across Dublin Bay at a sedate pace. After both boats had returned to the marina we invited Fia and his crew Kati and Stefano onboard Spirit for tea and biscuits and enjoyed chatting with these very friendly, helpful people telling them all about the flying rings campaign. They were all extremely concerned about the seals and fired up to spread the message of the campaign.

The campaign cruising chute

Flying the chute in Dublin Bay Photo by Fia OCaoimh

From left Kati, Fia and Stefano

The following day we sailed in fair weather and a moderate following wind around the impressive Howth peninsula towards Malahide, a short hop northwards. We goose-winged the sails, one to either side, through Howth Sound, a shallow, tricky stretch of water between Howth and the beautifully wild, Eye of Ireland island. The channel into Malahide estuary and marina shallows to a depth of one metre at low water, insufficient for Spirit, so we needed tide up to get in without grounding. The tide was rising; it's always a good idea to plan for this in shallow waters so a boat will be lifted if it accidentally grounds, and we made it safely in with a least depth of two and a half metres (Spirit's keel extends 1.7m under the water level).

Strong winds were forecast for Wednesday, Friday and the weekend. It looked like we had a small weather window on Thursday to sail north the 50 nautical miles to Ardglass with a very early start of 4.00am to catch the tide. However, when we checked the forecasts late Wednesday afternoon, the predicted wind had risen to 'strong southerly winds up to gale force' on Thursday afternoon and evening. We could not identify any easy bolt holes on the route either: Drogheda has limited berths and looked shallow; Carlingford Lough, the almanac advised, is open to the south and it can be rougher in the Lough than outside with strong southerly winds. These strong winds, which were caused by the tail end of tropical storm Alex, tracking across the Atlantic, put paid to our plans as we didn't fancy a 10 hour passage in these conditions. Unfortunately, we also had to pay for the forecast; Malahide Marina is not cheap at 44 Euros a night so the decision to stay was to cost us over 200 Euros!

Despite the hit on our cruising budget I was hugely relieved we had made the decision to stay and enjoyed a wonderfully relaxed evening and a deep sleep. Richard too enjoyed the morning's lie in. The weather confirmed our decision to stay with mist, rain and wind most of that Thursday and unsettled conditions following with strong winds rising to gale force at times.

In between the squalls we explored the attractive, coastal town of Malahide. Set in a nature reserve estuary, unobtrusive trains pass along a viaduct behind the marina. Malahide Castle (in Irish, Caislean Mhullach Ide) is impressive and set in beautifully kept grounds with areas for wildlife and a butterfly house. Parts of the castle date back to the 12th century when Henry 11 granted the land and harbour to a knight, Richard Talbot. The estate remained with the Talbot family for almost 800 years until it was sold to the Irish State in 1975.

Malahide is well linked to Dublin by the DART train and is quite a holiday location. There are lots of boutique type cafés, restaurants and pubs in The Village, an area of little streets in the centre of town. The Dart also runs to Howth and we satisfied our curiosity one morning by taking the train there. We explored the harbour, seeing a huge bull grey seal near the fishing boats with his mate, and later took the popular and precipitous cliff top walk around the headland.

The weather finally allowed us to break free from Malahide on June 13th and continue northwards to the small fishing harbour and marina of Ardglass. As skipper I was in charge of passage planning. On this occasion, when I was trying to enter a waypoint just off the entrance to Ardglass Harbour, I could not see the 'X' mark appearing on the chart plotter. I called Richard to check my co-ordinates and he pointed out I had entered 54 degrees south rather than north: so my waypoint was in the Southern Ocean!

After a week of strong winds it was pleasant to find the sea calm and in fact we needed to motor-sail to keep a reasonable pace in a south, southwest force 3 wind. The trip was easy and uneventful giving us time to enjoy the Irish coast with the lofty peaks of the Mountains of Morne rising around Carlingford Lough, where the Irish Republic becomes Northern Ireland.

We reached the harbour entrance after a 10 hour passage, lowered and stowed the mainsail, then began to get out lines and fenders to secure Spirit to a pontoon in the marina. We knew space was limited and there were three other yachts heading in ahead of us, we were tiring and stress levels started to rise. The entrance was narrow and with the tide low the harbour walls rose dark and threatening around us. Then a head popped up and another – there were seals in the outer fishing harbour with a group lounging on the middle breakwater, for all the world looking as relaxed as a crowd of sun bathers! Coming in to moor is a busy time and I had no chance of taking any pictures of the seals. The next morning when I had the time they had all gone.

We really enjoyed our overnight stay in Ardglass. This little marina is run as a charity by a group of volunteers. A senior member welcomed us together with the marina cat and the facilities were cosy and comfortable with hot showers and armchairs to relax in. We also found the best fish and chip, veggie burger café of the trip so far.

Before leaving the next morning we chatted to Derek and Leah on their yacht Sprinter who we had met in Malahide. They are seasoned sailors who have been enjoying spring-summer cruising for the past 18 years and know the coasts of Britain well. With a fair tide and a southerly wind similar to the previous day, we soon passed Strangford Lough just a few miles north of Ardglass. Reputedly one of, if not the most, attractive loughs and nature reserves in the whole of Ireland, we would have liked to visit but realising how much delay a poor forecast could cause we felt the need to push on towards Scotland.

We were bound for Bangor, Northern Ireland and needed to reach Donaghadee Sound before the tide turned against us. At 2pm we were not far off the sound when I heard a very clear and deliberate voice calling through the ship's radio:

'Spirit of Space, Spirit of Space.'

I thought at first it must be Derek on Sprinter but it continued:

'This is Belfast Coastguard, over..'

I then thought it must be to do with clearing customs or, God forbid, our red diesel which the EU has outlawed for leisure vessels, but I held it together and answered clearly and politely:

'Belfast Coastguard, Belfast Coastguard' (you always repeat things on a ship's radio) 'this is Spirit of Space, Spirit of Space, over..'

It turned out that a woman had reported a boat that looked in difficulty near the shore and we were the closest vessel to the position given. The Coastguard was asking us to take a look and pass on any information. We scoured the beaches with our binoculars but could see nothing. As we started to change course to take a closer look he called back to say their land based team had found the boat and were satisfied there was no concern. He very politely thanked us for our assistance, gave us leave to continue our passage and thankfully we whisked through the Sound, tide with us, just in time.

Bangor Marina is large yet friendly with a complete range of facilities. We had visited once before perhaps twenty years ago and I was amazed back then to find a bathroom, complete with bath, within the ladies' washrooms. I thought it unlikely this would have survived but when I asked at the office the answer was 'Yes you'll find things haven't changed much and the bath is still there.' I took my first bath for over two months, a wonderful, relaxing luxury after only having access to showers.

Another joy at Bangor was our first ever sightings of black guillemots. We noticed a bird, similar to a guillemot but smaller, blacker with bright red feet, sitting near the gangway to the pontoons seemingly unperturbed by passers-by. During the course of the evening and following morning we saw several of these very cute birds and heard about Julian Greenwood who has studied them in the marina for the past 30 years and led the successful breeding programme there.

Black guillemot, Bangor marina

The weather forecast had given us a window the following day for crossing the Irish Sea to Scotland, with landfall at Campbeltown on the inside of the Mull of Kintyre, before the arrival of a series of more Atlantic fronts. A beautiful summer's morning greeted us and we were blessed with perfect sailing conditions: a steady force 3-4 south easterly wind on the beam and a slight sea. We enjoyed a whole passage sailing without resorting to the engine, wonderful! As we entered the channel into Campbeltown Loch passing Devaar Island to port, after the 8 hour passage, our resolve to anchor almost faltered in favour of the little harbour pontoons, but we stayed firm and dropped the hook in a deep 12 metres letting out all our 50 metres of chain, together with the long snubber, in preparation for the forthcoming onslaught of fronts. Hello Scotland!

Hoisting the Scottish courtesy flag in Campbeltown Loch

Three nights we spent at anchor in Campbeltown Loch whilst wind and rain drove through from the south-east, west and north-west and we heard of sun and 25 degrees in Norfolk! There were lulls here and there allowing us to dinghy the three quarters of a mile into harbour to explore the town, sometimes getting a wee bit wet. Spirit's anchor held firm throughout, the sea in the loch remained flat and we both slept well, although we needed the heating on in the evenings!

You may wonder how we entertained ourselves during the evenings spent on board in a constricted space, especially when we had no access to shore. We got into a routine with Richard carrying out essential boat jobs and me passage planning before preparing a meal. Replete and relaxed we read a lot, both fiction and nonfiction, and sometimes watched a film or programme we had previously downloaded (including the entire series of Last Tango in Halifax over the six months!). We choose not to have a TV on board. We both enjoy music and have a guitar and keyboard on Spirit which we played occasionally. In good weather we sat in the cockpit soaking in the surroundings; on clear evenings we watched the glittering stars wheel overhead in their clockwork majesty.

The Loch seemed quiet and remote at first, herons flew over, black guillemots swam and preened nearby, and a seal popped its head up on the first morning. However, over the course of our stay there were actually a lot of comings and goings of ships: a large survey vessel which was docked in the harbour left; a big fish factory ship came near us and discharged water before docking; another ship came in to load up with wood; the Tall Ship Thallasa arrived (possibly on a malt whisky tour); the Caledonian McBrayne, CalMac for short, ferry came in from Ardrossan departing the following morning; and the RNLI lifeboat came out on training manoeuvres. One evening we noticed the hillside along from us was dotted with lights despite the fact we had noticed nothing there during the day. Later, chatting with the volunteer in the Heritage Centre she advised it was a NATO base where fuel and oil are stored and that it had lately become more active.

Campbeltown is attractively situated at the head of the Loch and revolves around The Quays and Springbank Distillery, which Richard advises me from his previous experience is one of the best single malts in all of Scotland. We discovered the Heritage Centre and café, a quirky, friendly, exhibition centre with very good Wi-Fi and the smallest coffee cups and cakes we had ever seen! The Heritage Trail led us to unexpected treasures around the town including the bronze statue of Linda McCartney in the community garden made by locals in her memory.

After pouring over our charts, information about the Firth of Clyde and weather forecasts we decided to move on to Lamlash Bay on Arran as soon as the main fronts had passed through. Although the wind was still forecasted to be a strong force 5-6 it was blowing towards Arran which meant a mainly downwind and therefore relatively comfortable sail, which it was with only our genoa raised. Though, arriving at Lamlash itself the wind lived up to its local reputation and whistled down the mountains, funnelling into the bay just where the mooring buoys were, one of which we had decided to hook up to. We managed to lasso the buoy on the first attempt then grappled with our mooring hook for many more trying to get a line through the buoy's top securing hoop, finally succeeding. A single hander on a French yacht then arrived and attempted the same. In the strong winds he was really struggling, leaning overboard to try and hold the buoy with his boat hook, impossible! We were quite worried about him and shouted our suggestion to use a lasso instead. Luckily, this worked and he showed his gratitude by coming over in his dinghy and helping us secure a second safety line to our buoy.

I was very keen to visit Holy Island in Lamlash Bay which is the home of a Tibetan Buddhist community and has its own Marilyn, a hill with a peak of 150m or more, this one is 314m. A ferry takes day visitors the mile across the bay to the island but discovering whether and when it was running was a bit of a challenge. Eventually, we found details online which informed us they were fully booked. I must have looked very disappointed because Richard said, 'No worries we'll go across in our own dinghy'. We fuelled up, put on our waterproofs and life jackets, set off and made it. Funnily enough, we met the ferry man at the island's jetty. He was very friendly and helpful advising us where to walk and offering to stand by if needed on our return trip – given the wind yesterday I was a bit apprehensive. We had an amazing walk up the Marilyn in beautiful sunshine meeting some of the non-human wild goat residents and enjoying stupendous views. Holy Island has a very special atmosphere and we felt very lucky to have been able to visit on such a lovely day. The following day we planned to leave beautiful Arran to explore deeper into the Firth of Clyde.

8

The Kyles of Bute, Crinan Canal and What's in a Date?

JUNE 20TH, 2022

I awoke at 6am to a blue skied, calm, sunny morning in Lamlash Bay – it was one of those perfect moments that make all the ups and downs of sailing worthwhile. I raised the Buddhist prayer flags I had been kindly given before setting off on our voyage, in recognition of Holy Isle and the community there.

Part of our planning for this trip had been to reduce our marina stays to roughly one a week. We needed this stop to plug into shore power, top up our batteries, fill the water tank, enjoy a proper shower and do the laundry. On this visit we also needed to buy a gas canister for the cooker, our second so far since we had set off, and we had arranged with the marina to collect some electrical equipment that Richard had pre-ordered.

The distances in the Firth of Clyde are not great; it was only 15 miles to Largs Marina on the mainland below Glasgow. We motor sailed in the calm to start with and saw the smooth grey backs of harbour porpoises arching gently in the water. The wind then picked up from the west and we had a cracking beam reach sail up Hunterston Channel, between the mainland and the Cumbrae Islands, to the marina.

Largs is another big marina with all facilities and mod cons. It's part of the Yacht Haven group which includes two marinas in the Solent at Lymington and Neyland, where we stayed in Milford Haven, but it has a price tag to suit! The staff were particularly friendly and helpful and the marina hosts a number of sailing events over the year.

The Fife Regatta had just ended, (a sailing competition for yachts designed by the Fife family from 1812 to 1944), and we saw some of the yachts which had travelled to Largs for the event from all over. This family of Scottish boat builders produced some of the most beautiful and fast wooden sailing yachts the world had ever seen. The sight of a Fife racing yacht under full sail still takes your breath away with its sleek, elegant hull shape and vast spread of canvas. Three generations of the family ran this business from the village of Fairlie on the banks of the Clyde Estuary which is next to Largs. We asked the marina staff if there were any original boat sheds left that we could visit but, disappointingly, were told that the entire site had been sold in the 1980s and demolished for re-development.

Another event had just started at Largs with Cornish Shrimpers, their skippers and crew gathering for 10 days of friendly racing, cruises in company and social events. The Cornish Shrimper is a modern, fibreglass, traditionally-styled sailing boat based upon gaff rigged fishing boats. Only 19 feet in length and weighing just over one tonne, these boats have cosy accommodation for two people (or one man and his dog). These little trailer-sailers were in complete juxtaposition to the thoroughbred Fifes. We only know all this because I bumped into Michael and his gorgeous sheep dog Jake in the marina laundry. Michael kindly explained how to work the washing machines whilst Jake slept, oblivious, in the corner. The following day we both met this intrepid pair and I introduced Richard to them.

Michael explained how he had trailed his Shrimper up to the West Coast of Scotland some weeks before and had sailed his pocket size boat from Oban to the islands of Eigg, Muck, Coll and Tiree, then along the Crinan Canal to reach the Firth of Clyde. No small feat for a sizeable yacht but extraordinary for such a small vessel and single handed to boot! Michael is ex-navy and evidently a very experienced sailor with a good weather eye. He gave us valuable advice about sailing in the Hebrides and where to visit. Actually, Michael was talking to me whilst Jake was keeping Richard busy throwing his tennis ball for him (Jake's ball not Richard's!).

The famed Kyles of Bute were almost in reach. Leaving Largs the next day having completed all our 'top up' chores, we anchored overnight at Port Ballantyne, on the eastern side of the Isle of Bute, then entered East Kyle, the hills rising around us. We picked up a visitor mooring, just past the CalMac ferry, belonging to the Hotel Colintraive. There is no charge for the mooring but you are expected to have a meal at the hotel, a regular arrangement in these parts. We duly rang and booked, ascertaining that they were open for drinks in the afternoon. We just needed to dinghy over.

I had read advice about where to land the dinghy from the Cruising Association's 'CAptain's Mate', a very useful app giving local information. One of the reports advised landing on the ferry slip but timing it for when the ferry had left or when it had stopped running for the day. We decided to paddle rather than use the outboard as it did not look far and the tide was not running too fast. We waited and waited for the ferry to leave then paddled to the ramp ready to run the dinghy ashore and out of the way. As we arrived a figure in a high vis jacket strode down the slip and advised us we could not land there and would have to go some distance away from the ferry. We tried to negotiate with this fearsome lady explaining that where she wanted us to go was too far to row and we would have to go back to our boat to collect our outboard. Well, she was having none of this! I urged Richard to comply and we pulled off, noticing the ferry was making its approach. In the end we fitted the outboard, had to fill it with fuel and found a disused slip just beyond the ferry ramps.

The hotel owner commiserated about our ferry experience and settled us into comfy sofas with welcome hot mugs of coffee and chocolate. I left Richard to recover his composure and walked along the single track road by the side of the Kyle catching glimpses of the Burnt Isles, islets just up from Colintraive. I was practising my script for a zoom interview arranged for that evening to talk about the seal campaign. On returning I discovered Richard strumming a guitar he had found in the bar. He admitted being a bit nervous earlier on as the owner's wife and their daughter had come to listen and 'dance' to his playing, the daughter being all of nine months old!

That evening we set up Spirit's saloon for the interview. Preparing and practising my script was invaluable and I was able to explain how I was sailing around Britain to raise awareness and describe clearly how the seals were getting entrapped in flying rings. I also gave the message to please play with solid frisbees rather than rings on beaches and near waterways.

Preparing to set off the following morning we heard a strange sloshing noise outside which was getting louder. Looking out, to our astonishment, we saw the beautiful paddle steamer Waverley, with its red, black and white funnels passing right by us! Waverley is one of the last working steam paddle ships in the world. It used to be based in the Solent and now offers a variety of trips in the Firth of Clyde including along the Kyles of Bute. Her maiden voyage was in 1947.

Our passage that day was the shortest yet. The tiny harbour of Caladh is just one mile further on from Colintraive through the Burnt Isles, at the foot of Loch Riddon. It is highly recommended as a very attractive anchorage and turned out for us to be the jewel of the Kyles. Nestled in behind the tiny wooded island Eilean Dubh, the harbour is a mini bay with a few houses set in grassy woodland with steep hillsides rising behind. The harbour can be popular and we feared there would be no space. It was actually practically deserted with a few little boats on moorings and no one else anchored there. The day was still and warm with cloud breaking into sunshine in the afternoon. At lunchtime some boats did arrive, it was a group of the Cornish Shrimpers having a leisurely sail and enjoying a lunch stop at Caladh. It was lovely to see them, though no Michael and Jake arrived. I took myself off for a good walk along part of the Loch Lomond Colway trail while Richard, avoiding any threat of inland midges, stayed on board for boat jobs and guitar practice. The Shrimpers left and much later one little sailing yacht arrived and anchored for the night. We were watching herons hunting from the rocks well into evening, it being light so late this far north.

Peace and calm in Caladh Harbour

We had been watching the weather and knew that a change was due with strong south-southeast winds heralding the arrival of more Atlantic fronts affecting Northern Ireland and north west Scotland over the weekend. We decided to seek shelter in East Loch Tarbert, a heritage village with a well-protected natural harbour, marina pontoons and visitor moorings. The wind had already picked up when we set off and we motored against it in West Kyle eventually rounding the exposed Ardlamont Point. It was then a calmer run under our genoa up to Tarbert, with the wind behind us. We were glad to reach shelter and, resisting the lure of the marina, picked up a mooring buoy just off the pontoons, for half the price.

We found Tarbert small, down to earth and attractive in a fishing village sort of way. The few shops, Co-op and comfortable café Ca'Dor, nestle around the harbour. Sea birds, herons and ducks feed, gather and roost on the islets and rocks, which rise up in the middle of the harbour channel. The moorings are a great place to watch them all and hear them at the start and end of the day. East Tarbert is situated at the top of the Mull of Kintyre peninsula. A narrow strip of land joins the town with West Loch Tarbert, a gateway to the West Coast of Scotland. We climbed up to the ruins of Tarbert Castle which, originally built as a hill fort, was repaired and extended by the Scottish king, Robert the Bruce, from 1325 when he realised the importance of protecting the isthmus.

The first time we paddled the dinghy ashore and landed on the nearest pontoon we found some of the Cornish Shrimpers had arrived including Michael and Jake. Jake immediately searched for his tennis ball in Michael's rucksack, which was in his boat's cockpit and brought it to Richard. I took my camera out to capture the scene but was too slow, so Michael set up the ball inside his rucksack for a second take. I aimed my camera at Jake and Michael advised 'Don't point the camera; he doesn't like his picture being taken!' So I waited till Jake had his head deep inside the rucksack before clicking! Jake looked disappointed that it was not safe to throw his ball on the pontoon, but we had a good catch up with Michael and heard what all the Shrimpers had been up to.

Strong onshore winds started to work into the moorings area of East Loch Tarbert along with some downpours. The movement resulted in our mooring buoy repeatedly banging against Spirit's hull. We decided to move into the greater shelter of the marina for our last night, bliss! Our next leg involved the transit of the Crinan Canal to reach the Highlands and islands of Scotland's West Coast. This would be a trip of two sentiments: I was looking forward to the calm of an inland waterway; Richard was losing sleep with worry about the potential damage to Spirit in the locks.

We left Tarbert on Monday June 27th after the fronts had blown through and motor-sailed up to the sea lock at Ardrishaig (pronounced Ardrishon) to enter the Crinan Canal. This 9 mile long canal conveniently connects the Firth of Clyde with Crinan providing a short passage to the Hebrides instead of taking the long detour south around the Mull of Kintyre. Unusually for canals the Crinan is navigable by sailing boats with their deep drafts and masts raised. We had booked and paid for our transit licence online, with an entry time of 12pm and were waved into an open and empty lock as soon as we arrived.

Now, canals with their locks are like marmite, you either love 'em or hate 'em. There is the calm and peace of the canal winding through attractive countryside with close views of wildlife and then there are the locks: big rocky structures with gigantic wooden gates and tons of water gushing in and out, ready to knock your boat about and cause untold damage. Not to speak of the midges. I love them, canals that is, Richard hates them, or so we found out during the next four days!

The first lock was worrying for us both as we were not used to them. When ascending you have to get your boat lines secure on bollards several feet above you. Thankfully, the very friendly and helpful staff helped us and operated the first two locks which were also automated, not too bad. Richard still needed his first slice of Battenburg cake, the sugar hit helping to relieve his stress. We motored a short way up the canal and moored in a quiet, pleasant spot just before Oakfield Bridge near the only small town on the canal of Lochgilphead. We had decided to stay here the following day whilst a bucket full of rain was due to come through and we also needed to fill our outboard can at the petrol station. Bill, one of the canal staff, cycled up, kindly connected us to the shore power and asked when we would like to leave. We walked into town, found the recommended veggie café, Smiddy's, and then relaxed on board watching the many swallows swoop and dive over the canal catching insects and showing their beautiful iridescent blue backs.

It poured all the next day as forecasted and the winds, hardly perceptible on the canal, were so strong we heard that the CalMac ferries had stopped running. We had found out that the local swimming pool, plus café, was next to the petrol station and planned for me to have a swim alongside filling our fuel can and having a cuppa. At 11.30am my sister Phil sent a message about getting ready to meet us on Mull, a rendezvous we had arranged back in February, which included a day's wildlife tour. I replied:

'Yes, I can't believe it's less than 2 weeks till we see you.'

I had noted her arrival for Sunday July 10th in my diary and the wildlife tour was booked for the 13th.

She replied very quickly:

> 'Less than 2 weeks??? It's 5 days. The ferry gets in at 4.30pm on Sunday 3rd!'

My heart missed several beats, oh my goodness I had completely messed up the dates! I put my head in my hands. Richard and I spent the rest of the day sorting out this calamity. Luckily, Crinan was only 40 odd miles from Tobermory on Mull, we could manage that in time, crossing fingers for the weather. The wildlife tour was another matter, it was difficult enough to find a slot when I booked back in February, what chance did we have now? After a lot of research and leaving messages, by the end of the day Richard had managed to book another tour for us with Andrew Tomison through a work contact he had. Disaster and disappointment had been averted and an important lesson learnt: check arrangements, double check and then check once more! Through all this Richard suggested we still kept to our plan as the swim would help to calm my nerves, which it did.

The weather had cleared the next morning and we waited hopefully for Bill to show and open the bridge for 9am. Quarter past and no Bill. I managed to get through to the canal office and they said 'Ah yes I'll tell him, he's just here'! Bill duly cycled up to open the swing bridge and assured that the next lock keeper would look after us. The next two flights of locks were the main event, four up and five down leaving two automated ones to finish. We arrived at the idyllic scene at Cairnbaan: a hotel and pretty cottages alongside the first lock. There was no lock keeper in sight. I walked up past some of the upper locks, saw a boat leaving and returned to Richard suggesting we should try to work the lock. We opened the sluices to let the water out then tried to open the gates, no chance – they were not giving way. The lock keeper then turned up, he said he did not know we were coming, and advised we had not fully closed the top gate sluices so water was continuing to flow in keeping the gates closed, how embarrassing! He was extremely helpful and advised that two other boats were on their way and if we did not mind waiting we could all go through together, the advantage being they could help us operate the locks. Eventually the boats arrived and Richard's nightmare began!

Richard shares his experience of tackling the 9 locks:

'Jenny scaled the ladder commando style to take up the lines on the first lock. She then got stranded up on the quay, leaving me to run back and forth trying to handle both the bow and stern lines on Spirit whilst she surged around against the lock wall out of control. Boat two then squeezed in behind us with her anchor perilously close to our self-steering gear; midges appeared and attacked me, especially as the water level went down. I had to manoeuvre Spirit into the narrow locks on my own, getting her close enough to the wall so that lines could be thrown up to Jenny on the quay. There were a couple of bangs and heart stopping moments but thankfully the only part that sustained damage was the wooden fender board which was replaceable.'

Lock horror!

We realised in hindsight that we had too few fenders for protecting Spirit in a lock, we had not set our lines up efficiently back to the cockpit onto winches and there was no way we could have managed on our own securing the lines and opening the gates. The crews of the other boats, a mixture of Scottish, Northern Irish and English chaps were a gift from heaven. They had their system down to a fine art having transited the canal several times before. Richard still needed more slices of Battenburg and a full afternoon cleaning Spirit to calm him down!

The canal itself was wonderfully undeveloped and quiet, the banks full of wildflowers and grasses. There were lily patches promising a show of flowers, and herons perched here and there on overhanging branches. Reaching the end of the canal at Crinan after passing Moine Mhor nature reserve was spectacular with a completely different look and feel to the Firth of Clyde. Wild, remote Scottish islands stretched into the distance with the peaks of Mull beyond. On the far side of Crinan Loch stood Duntruin Castle which is the oldest continuously occupied castle on mainland Scotland, built in the 13th century by the MacDougall clan. The clear, golden light of the evening sun brought everything into sharp relief.

We spent a night above lock 14 where the midges were reportedly less bother than down in the basin and bought our new friends a round of drinks in the cosy bar of the Crinan Hotel. They had recommended quinine as an antidote to midge bites but we suspected this was just an excuse for them to enjoy a number of gin and tonics! By this stage Richard was keen to try any remedy so we downed a number of tonic waters during the evening. We had a great time listening to their sailing stories and antics and they were very helpful in pointing out must see places on the West Coast of Scotland.

The Crinan Canal is an engineering feat started in 1771 by James Watt and finally completed with the help of James Paterson in 1809. The canal made it easier for goods to be transported to and from the Clyde to the west coast. Puffer boats powered by coal fired steam engines, plied their trade taking coal, fish and livestock back and forth. A whole community grew up along the banks of the canal.

I spent our last day taking a walk in Crinan Wood, a temperate rainforest remnant of the ancient Atlantic oak woods, and passage planning for our trip to Mull back on board. Tides on the West Coast of Scotland run strongly between some of the islands, and rocks abound. Our passage to Mull would also take us past the notorious Corryvreckan, a narrow strait between the islands of Jura and Scarba. It has one of the largest permanent whirlpools on earth and is also one of the most dangerous stretches of water around the British Isles! I poured over the Clyde Cruising Club Sailing directions to find a safe route past Corryvrechan, through the Sound of Luing then into the more open and easier waters of the Firth of Lorne and Sound of Mull. The weather forecast promised a calm if cloudy day with possible rain showers. I woke for a time at 4.30am with some anxiety about the passage then fell asleep until 7. In the event the planning was more stressful than the actual passage which passed smoothly without trauma. We saw seals in the distance, pale shapes on dark rocks, and the occasional individual popped their heads up; there were frequent groups of guillies including black guillemots and a large group of shags. I've never seen so many swimming together. The wind was light and gave us a little help but we needed the engine to reach Mull. Tobermory was a welcome sight at 7pm in the evening after our 40 mile passage. We had arrived in the nick of time to make our promised rendezvous with my sister Phil.

It was the beginning of July and amazingly we had been away for three of our six month trip. We were where we had planned to be, up on the West Coast of Scotland, having covered 830 sea miles, we had also spent a lot more on fuel and marinas than planned. In fact the experience of time felt quite different from our previous shore-based lives. When planning trips at home we have a good idea how long it's going to take, which roads we will drive along and generally know some of the landmarks and scenery on the way. These landmarks anchor the journey in a timescale: we know how far we have travelled and when we are nearly there. At sea it was completely different, especially as we were making passages along stretches of the coast we had never been to. Sailing on Spirit was not unlike stepping aboard a magic carpet, everything was fresh and new, we had no idea of what it would be like where we ended up and the sea itself was constantly changing. Time seemed flexible, recalling where we were even the previous day seemed a very long time ago.

9

Isle of Mull, Eagles and Gateway to the Small Isles

JULY 3RD, 2022

Phil and I had three full days to make the most of her trip to Mull whilst Richard was busy working on boat jobs he had planned and been unable to complete before our somewhat busy departure. Mull is a big island and Phil's car was an absolute boon. The first morning we rose early to drive to Salen, halfway down the coast towards Craignure where the car ferry lands from Oban, to join Andrew Tomison and six others for the wildlife tour.

Andrew has lived on the island for 33 years and has an extensive knowledge and love of the wildlife that lives and visits there. He told us about the diverse range of habitats and wealth of food sources on land and sea in Mull, as well as the challenges arising from the vested interests of farmers and logging companies. The numbers of red deer are very high, a result of human interference with the eco-system. For example, all large predators of deer have been hunted to extinction, and this has resulted in large areas being unable to sustain woods and forest because the deer eat the saplings. Deer fencing is erected to allow woods to grow and 2,000 deer are culled annually.

We realised over the course of the day that a good wildlife guide knows the habits, routines and territories of the local animals and where it's possible to stop a minibus at good viewing points. This is crucial on Mull where most of the roads are single track and you are not allowed to park in the passing places. Before we set off Andrew asked what we would most like to see, the answers were predictable: white tailed eagles, golden eagles and otters! He said he would do his best but with all the knowledge in the world, sightings of these elusive creatures were not guaranteed. Some of the other birds are easier to see and we had good views of arctic terns, eider ducks, oyster catchers, sand pipers, herons, a stone chat, Canada and greylag geese. We stopped at many, many places where there was a possibility of a sighting, for example of hen harriers, but they were either not about or Andrew caught a glimpse then they disappeared!

However, the knowledge Andrew had of eagles' nests did pay off and quite early on, south of Craignure, he showed us the location of the eyrie of a pair of white tailed eagles. High up in a copse of conifers a large nest of sticks, (three metres across he said), was just visible and as we arrived a white tailed eagle, one of the pair, flew over us showing its very broad wings with finger tips. The size of the bird was evident when it was mobbed by a crow which was tiny in comparison. It was an amazing sight and a first for Phil and me. Local sheep farmers, of which there are few in Mull, have concerns about these eagles preying on lambs and an arrangement has been made for this pair whereby the farmer feeds them meat during the lambing season. This has cut the numbers of lambs taken substantially. There had been two chicks in the nest but we could not catch a glimpse of them until we drove to a loch on the far side of the nest. From there, with binoculars, we could just make out the back of a well grown chick standing in the nest.

Looking for eagles, Mull

We spent a long time watching cliffs around the nest of a pair of golden eagles with no sightings and similarly with another white tailed eagle nest, but here some of us were lucky to catch a glimpse of the chick before it hunkered down. The day was windy with frequent drizzle and showers, not the best conditions for seeing eagles. Andrew explained that the 'goldies' were most probably sheltering on a cliff edge watching us from afar. We did have luck in seeing short-eared owls flying though. Some distance away across rough fields, we saw them just above the ground, pale shapes flapping their wings almost in slow motion.

Well on in the day, Andrew took us down to the edge of a sea loch to look for otters. He, and all of us, scoured the shoreline searching for movement. The conditions were right with the sea at half tide leaving the rocky, seaweed clad shore exposed and the promise of crustaceans and fish to catch. Time and again we paused, no otter in sight, until Phil and a couple of others noticed a movement in the water – a fish jumping? It disappeared as soon as they glimpsed it. A woman was walking along the road, binoculars in hand and said she had just seen an otter. We stopped and sure enough in a few minutes, a female otter surfaced chomping on something. We watched quietly, without getting out of the van. Andrew explained that the otter can see movement ashore, additionally if the profile of the shoreline is different from what she expects she will scarper. Also, if she sees a threat, she will not bring her catch ashore which she needs to do if it is large or if she is taking it to feed her kits who will be secure in their holt up in the woods on the far side of the road.

We watched as the otter surfaced with food she had caught then dived, arching her dark, brown, agile body into the sea. She worked gradually up the shoreline and we kept sight of her for so long that we parked behind some bushes so we did not spook her, and had our lunch. For me this was another wonderful first, I had so wanted to see a wild otter and here she was relaxed in her natural setting.

Our final sighting was another first for most of us. Andrew took us to the location of another golden eagle nest. The setting was dramatic, high up in dark granite cliffs above a sea loch with Munroes, Scottish mountains, behind including Ben Mhor, the highest on Mull. We could see no sight of a nest from the road with or without binoculars but Andrew had two telescopes and from a distance of half a mile he trained them both on the nest. He looked and said the chick was there. I looked and looked and saw nothing, as did Phil until, eventually, with help, we could see the 'chick' on the left hand side of the nest when it turned its head. It was huge! Its outer back feathers were dark brown but its head was still covered in pale down and after a while I saw it stand and stretch a wing. The whole group was elated: smiling and chatty with this treasure of an experience.

Andrew had worked very hard during the day to find wildlife for the group to see and marvel at: half of us were lucky enough to see an adder curled up basking, despite the rainy, chill day, before it felt our vibration and slid away. He also told us about some of the history of the places we passed including the island Inch Kenneth which was owned by the Mitford family, the six daughters divided by their fascist and communist views.

For most of our six days in Tobermory the weather was misty, drizzly and rainy but on the second day of Phil's visit we enjoyed a warm sunny morning and donned our wetsuits to swim in the sea at beautiful Calgary Bay, yes Calgary in Canada was named after this little Scottish bay. After our dip we walked around the bay and saw a seal bob up to take a look around. As we returned through the car park a father was walking down to the beach with his two children, one of whom was holding a flying ring. I approached them and asked if I could have a word about the seals. I explained the problem to them all and gave them a leaflet, reassuring the children that the seals featured had been rescued and were now alright.

Engaging children has been an important part of the campaign. Over 100 pupils engaged in project work that I sent out to coastal schools in 2019. The children responded magnificently: their comments showed a strong feeling and connection with the seals and their wish to help them. They also made the connection with the general problem of plastic pollution in the sea.

Six-year-olds wrote:

'They put their heads through, get stuck and can't get them off'

'I was sad and angry to learn this...always pick up plastik'

'Don't chuck rings at the beach' 'No toys in the sea'

'Please help me' 'Don't let me die' (Answering: 'What is the seal asking you to do, or not do?')

By a 10-year-old girl:

'I did not know that it was a problem but now I want to help and let people know'

By an 11-year-old boy:

'sad as somebody was lazy which nearly cost the seal its life' (Answering how do the pictures in the leaflet make you feel?')

*

Leaving Calgary Bay we wended through steep, beautiful woods, along the sculpture trail of Calgary Art in Nature finding a lovely café and gallery to relax in before heading back to Tobermory.

Back on board each day, we found Richard progressing with his main job: repairing a scrape we had sustained on Spirit's upper hull. He had also managed to fit in some café breaks, a long overdue haircut, and helped out a neighbouring boat with their electrical problem which they kindly rewarded with a bottle of red wine.

On Phil's final day we experienced the small aquarium next to the marina, where all the sea life is local and 'visits' for a month before being released back to the wild. Later we walked from Tobermory south along the coastal path to Aros park with its thundering waterfalls, serene lily-clad lake and moss-covered trees.

On Thursday July 7th we waved goodbye to Phil and went to provision up Spirit and top up our water before hopping over to a sheltered anchorage in Loch Droma Bhuide, which lies off the larger Loch Sunart. We needed to make a plan for the next few days before returning to Tobermory for the original wildlife tour I had booked. In the loch there was no Wi-Fi, phone signal or habitation. We were surrounded by hills in the ultimate wild, sailing setting. Thrown onto our own resources we read, wrote and enjoyed the peace.

We decided to relax for a few days and moved up to the little bay of Salen on the north side of Loch Sunart. On the way we managed to get a mobile signal and rang Jan who owns the pontoon and moorings there. It was lucky we caught her as we found there were just two moorings unbooked. This really was an attractive spot with a very friendly atmosphere. Jan supplied us with a summary of local walks and the couple running the local shop cum mini café welcomed us in. This had just two tables, proper coffee and sumptuous home-baked cakes. Even the sun came out for us on the two days we were there. We enjoyed some of the local walks and Richard had time to finish another boat job: fitting new cockpit speakers to replace our defunct ones, we were both happy!

It may seem that we ate mainly in cafés, in fact all of our evening meals were cooked on board and we prepared snacks to eat on passage. I had taken a full locker of dried food – pasta, rice, fruit, nuts, cereals and flour – stored in unbreakable plastic sweet jars. Another locker held an array of tinned food, some of which we still had by the end of our cruise. Fresh food, fruit and vegetables we bought on the way. As ship's cook I prepared simple meals on our two ring gas cooker with a grill and very handy little oven. Bakes of pasta or rice and vegetables, pasta with a sauce, and quiches with salad were the order of the day. After a long passage hot roast veggie sausages and baked beans could be knocked up in five minutes to satisfy our hunger. I'd planned to make my own yoghurt and bread but somehow never found the time. Puddings were a welcome treat with pancakes a firm favourite and passage snacks were generally rolls filled with cheese, peanut butter or hummus.

We planned to anchor in another little bay before returning to Tobermory but a strong southerly wind was forecast and we feared all the buoys in the harbour there would soon be taken by boats seeking shelter, so we returned early in preparation for our wildlife day. We picked up a buoy and found ourselves next to Josie and Ben on their Sweden yacht Opora. We had been bumping into them since Arklow in Ireland: at Bangor, Arran, Port Ballantyne, and Salen! We finally got together for a proper chat on board Opora and Richard found in Ben a fellow sailor who is even more obsessive than him about not scratching his woodwork and keeping his boat clean. It was their first season of extended sailing since retirement, just like us, and it was very interesting to compare experiences. Richard though, came away from the visit crestfallen that he needed to raise his game, this did not bode well for the rest of Spirit's crew!

On Wednesday morning, July 13th, we rose in good time, donned our walking boots and waterproofs, rain and showers being forecast again, and took the 9am double decker bus, quite an experience on the single track roads, from Tobermory to Craignure to meet Peter Hall our wildlife guide for the day. We found the nearby café open and were enjoying drinks and a butty when I saw Peter walking past. He joined us and the rest of the day flowed on in a very relaxed way. We had the luxury of Peter and his comfortable car to ourselves as Phil's place was not taken and the woman who had booked the fourth space had unfortunately just tested positive for covid, a real shame for her.

Peter has been a keen bird watcher for many years starting in Wolverhampton where he and his wife were members of a local group. When they moved to Mull 23 years ago he started a local bird group and the wildlife guiding grew from that. He and Andrew, who took Phil and I out the previous week, are good friends and carry out wildlife recces together. Peter was very easy to be with, he is a very friendly chap and knew practically everyone we met or drove past.

The sightings we had of eagles were quite amazing: Richard spotted the first, a white-tailed eagle flying just over the nearby pine trees as we left a hide. Peter then took us to a copse of conifers where a pair have a nest and showed us how to scan the tops with our binoculars to look for an adult and ... there it was! Watching and preening, it was probably resting having already fed its chick which was on the nest hidden deep in the wood. We had yet another sighting of a white-tailed eagle which was standing on a tiny rocky islet in a sea loch. We watched it take off, circle up high and way above the opposite hillside before landing again on the islet. The white tail was very visible and made it easy to identify compared to a golden eagle.

We also visited the nest of the golden eagles I had seen with Phil and the chick was still there, not due to fledge for about another three weeks. As we were watching one of the parents landed with prey, one minute nothing then suddenly it appeared! We were very lucky, Peter said people have stayed watching the nest for a whole day and not seen an adult bird. Just as we were getting ready to leave the parent bird flew off but then perched on the cliff not far away. Eventually Peter managed to train his scope on it and we enjoyed a further view, this was all from a distance of half a mile with no disturbance to the eagles. Through Peter's car skylight we later saw another golden eagle soaring above us, taking not one flap of its broad wings to stay aloft, incredible.

Peter identified many other birds for us including common sandpipers, female eiders with their young, wheatears including young ones, a skylark, who was enjoying a dust bath nearby, a linnet, meadow pipit, mergansers, greylag geese, arctic terns, whinchat and rock dove. In the hide we enjoyed watching a harbour seal hauled out and relaxing on the rocks, a heron stalking food and a curlew. We searched and searched for otters but on this day found none, they are elusive. We returned exhausted and grateful for all the wildlife we had seen, for Peter's company and for the knowledge he had shared with us.

The harbour seal, well camouflaged, photo taken from the hide.

During our protracted stay in Tobermory I was able to talk to the Hebridean Whale and Dolphin Trust and Mull Sealife Tours about the campaign I was promoting to keep seals safe from plastic flying rings. They didn't know that seals had been getting entangled in these rings and were very concerned. They offered their support in spreading the message. We also popped into the local chandlery which, unfortunately, had flying rings for sale. The owner was unaware of the potential danger these rings could pose for seals if inadvertently lost or discarded on the beach or in the sea. She was shocked and said we had spoilt her day. I could understand how she felt. Some of the people I have talked to have been unable to hold back their tears when they saw the photos of the seals with rings embedded into their necks. When I first heard about the seals getting caught and saw the extent of their injuries I lost sleep worrying about them, going over in my mind how much they were suffering.

We planned to move out of Tobermory the following day, Thursday July 14th and continue our sea adventures northwards. The fair tide started late so in the morning we topped up our provisions, water and fuel and even managed to do the laundry before heading for Rum, one of the Inner Hebridean Small Isles, the others being Muck, Eigg and Canna. Leaving the Sound of Mull to the north involves rounding Ardnamurchan Point, the most westerly point of mainland Britain and quite a rite of passage for sailors. The shelter of the Sound is left behind exposing open seas to the west. Even with a fair forecast the waves beyond the Point held a slight Atlantic swell and felt different. A northwesterly wind was on our nose to Ardnamurchan then it gradually backed west and south west giving us a good sail all the way up to Rum. We soon saw and passed Muck with Eigg rising dark and forbidding behind it. Sailing up the Sound of Rum the sea assumed a lake-like calm in the shelter of the island until we turned west into the anchorage of Loch Scresort where it whistled down the mountainside. We resisted the temptation of picking up the last free mooring buoy and anchored in a depth of six metres towards the head of the loch.

Exhausted after our passage we slept well and no alarm was set as we had an afternoon departure to take the tide towards Skye next day. We could not tell what the land held from the sea: Rum looked quite bare from a distance but when we explored ashore the following morning there were woods, burns and a number of different dwellings including a bunkhouse, holiday huts, local shop and community hall. It was beautifully quiet and offered retreat, wildlife and mountainous walking. The whole island is a National Nature Reserve. The sun came out lightening the mountain's shadows and we walked up beside one of the island's burns towards a viewing point, returning to the shop to enjoy hot drinks and doughnuts, a morsel of which was gratefully received by the shop's dog! Returning to the quay we were slightly alarmed at how far the tide had retreated leaving our dinghy high and dry on the rocks and seaweed. We scaled down the ladder in bare feet to retrieve and carry her a fair way to the sea.

Richard talking to the shop dog!

A gentle reach towards Skye

With the sun shining and a good westerly wind behind us we enjoyed a lovely sail to Skye. On the way and up the Sound of Sleat we were treated to the sight of Manx shearwaters gliding in big groups around us, making splashes in the sea as they dived for food. We reached our destination, the sheltered anchorage at Isleornsay, around 8pm. This natural harbour would give us good protection from the strong southerly wind due to blow up overnight. We dropped our anchor in a depth of nine metres and let out almost 50 metres of chain, with our long snubber, in preparation. We slept soundly and moved not an inch.

In the morning I looked out of the window towards the shore and saw an otter! It was surfacing then diving, working up the edge of the land, it was Richard's first sighting, my second – fantastic!

10

Skye and The Outer Hebrides

JULY 16TH, 2022

We had made it to Skye, one of the iconic islands of the Inner Hebrides that I had wanted to visit for many years. Isleornsay on the east side of the island is an attractive bay protected by the island of Ornsay with a tiny hamlet consisting of a little hotel, gallery and a handful of houses around its ancient stone jetty. We enjoyed two days of gentle walks, hearty soup in the hotel bar and an afternoon relaxing in the lounge, blog-writing and chatting to Freya and Kaz, local sailors, who we had just met whose boat, An Faoilean, was also moored in the bay.

The strong winds blew through and we were able to continue northwards up the Sound of Sleat. There were three challenges on this passage; passing through the narrow channel of Kyle Rhea, where the tides can run up to 8 knots at springs; going under Skye bridge, which links the mainland to the island; and navigating through rocky islets into Plockton, Loch Carron. I spent some time passage planning and entering waypoints into our electronic chart to aid our navigation. Tides are key in many parts of the Hebrides and we needed them with us, especially for Kyle Rhea and also for Skye Bridge. This gave us another late start and with sun and warmth forecast we decided to cross to Scaldaig Bay just across the sound for a possible swim. The beach here was made famous by the naturalist Gavin Maxwell in his book 'Ring of Bright Water'. This is where he brought up his pet otter from Iraq 'Mijbil', immortalising the animal through his writing.

The sea was freezing off the boat and there was a slight swell, so Richard stayed aboard keeping anchor watch whilst I paddled ashore in the dinghy. I found a patch of beach where the sand glittered and managed to swim for the first time on the trip without the second skin of a wet suit, despite the moon (non-stinging) jellyfish.

I do not know what happened with my passage planning but we had some tide with us approaching the narrows at Kyle Rhea then it went against us. Luckily, the current was slight and we managed to sail through, dodging the ferry which plies across this narrow channel, with very little engine help. The rest of the passage went smoothly and we successfully passed under Skye Bridge and identified the two white beacons marking the passage into Plockton where we dropped our anchor in between the outer moorings. Loch Carron on the mainland reminded us of a Swiss lake: we were surrounded by high wooded hills dotted with white houses, a 19th century 'castle' looked over the bay, and a train ran through the woods and over a bridge in the distance. It was all very beautiful.

The two days of our visit to Plockton were the hottest in England where temperatures rose to a worrying 40°c whilst we were experiencing only 22! The sun shone encouraging us to walk across the peninsula to Coral Beach and take a swim. The water was wonderfully clear, with patches of sand between wafting fronds of seaweed. With my snorkel

I could see little green crabs walking across the sand and hiding if they sensed my movement. The 'coral' on the beach is actually calcified seaweed. We learnt a little of the history of Plockton in the information centre back in the village, including the devastating effects of the clearances in the 18th and 19th centuries when landowners evicted crofters to make way for sheep farming, an occurrence oft repeated across the islands and Highlands. A few crofts and crofters have survived in Plockton and at least a part of their living is made from their land and animals. Paddling back to Spirit in the anchorage, the heavens opened and a deluge of rain hit us. We were soaked through, so the heating went on yet again to dry everything out!

Our passage the following day was towards Rona, another iconic Inner Hebridean island. Before setting off we took advantage of the opportunity to refill our water tank at the small floating dock used by fishermen and tripper boats. Manoeuvring ourselves alongside we were immediately accosted by the tripper boat skipper who had left his milk bottle suspended in the water to keep it cool overnight! Luckily, we had berthed without crushing it and he retrieved it, contents intact. The water hose kindly provided by a local resident was of the garden hose reel variety and it was located at the shore end of the pontoon. However, turning on the tap produced no water. The tripper boat captain kindly explained we needed to go into the garden of the first house on the left where we would find another tap to make the water flow. So far, so good. Pulling out the hose from the reel it was soon obvious that it was no way long enough to reach the boat. Not to be thwarted we cobbled together various connectors and by adding our own on-board hose it finally reached the tank.

Turning on the supply, water proceeded to spout out of the hose pipe at various points all along the quay with a dribble reaching the tank. Richard was still filling it when I returned from the village having bought bread and milk!

For the passage a fairly gentle wind was forecast to blow from the west-southwest then veer northwest. On leaving Plockton we motored with our mainsail up for the first few miles, expecting to unfurl the genoa and sail northwards with south or west still in the wind. However, as we passed the island of Eilean Mor ready to turn northwest we found the wind had already veered and was right on our nose. The wind strength had also increased and the sea became choppy. We almost changed course to seek shelter, but as we neared the island of Raasay the sea calmed in its lee and we were able to set a comfortable northerly course to Rona, sailing all the way. Passing through the narrow rocky channel of Caol Rona, between the northerly tip of Raasay and the south end of Rona, we saw an eagle flying above the cliff side of Raasay. I watched it land through the binoculars and saw its white tail. Later we heard from Bill, warden of Rona, that a pair of white-tailed eagles had a nest on that cliff. Just a mile up the coast we turned into the hidden harbour of Acarsaid Mhor (Gaelic for Large Harbour), once a hideaway for pirates and smugglers, and picked our way gingerly through the many rocks to pick up the last but one mooring, as there was precious little room for us to anchor.

Rona is only about five miles long and a mile wide, yet there are some native wooded areas and a varied population of wildlife including some red deer. The few rough tracks wend up and down its steep hills giving access to the island. Rona's history is well depicted in the museum – one of the derelict cottages now renovated, or at least re-roofed. Few people lived on Rona over the centuries but in 1843 George Rainy, a Scottish merchant, bought both Raasay and Rona and cleared many of the families from Raasay to make room for sheep. Some of these people moved to Rona raising the population to 180. They struggled to make a living on the much smaller and less fertile island. 1921 saw a group of Rona's men 'The Raasay Raiders' return to Raasay to reclaim their ancestral lands. They were tried and imprisoned but after a huge public outcry were released and their lands restored after the government bought Raasay and Rona. Most of the families returned to Raasay; just a few crofting families remained on Rona with the last leaving in 1943.

The anchorage of Arcarsaid Mhor on Rona, Spirit far right

The reduction in population on Rona relieved pressure on its woodland and there was some natural regeneration. To cut a very long and interesting story short the island was bought in 1992 by the current Danish owners Dorte Jensen and her husband Arne Fremmich who have done a great job in restoring more native woodland thus providing habitats for wildlife with the help of woodland grants. Interestingly, a group of red deer live on the island without apparent damage to the woods. Bill, the warden, told us that the deer are all hinds visited at courting time by stags who swim across from Raasay!

When we paddled to the pontoon to step ashore on Rona we expected hot showers, loos and a laundry at Rona Lodge, as described in our pilot book. Instead we found Bill the resident warden of 20 years who lives in the Lodge with his family. Bill informed us, with some glee we felt, there were no showers or any other facilities as they were too expensive to run for the few yachties who visited. He did though give us the time of day (whilst we longingly eyed up the mugs, biscuits and kettle in the bunkhouse to no avail) and told us about the island, the owners 'more friends than employers', and where to explore. He also had some impressive photos he had taken from his boat of two orcas (also known as killer whales although they are actually a species of dolphin), spotted off Rona. He has had only four sightings in 20 years. Bill has an evident love and concern for wildlife on land and in the sea and a down to earth, personal philosophy on the planet's challenges. We enjoyed listening to him.

Following up Bill's suggestions we discovered the derelict cottages, school and mission house of past crofters as well as two houses that have been renovated by the owners and are let for holidays. We met the current visitors, coincidentally from Sheffield, where I worked for many years. I discovered Church Cave an actual cave up above a rocky cove and place of worship for many years. Islanders would scramble down to the cave from the moor above and sit on rocks arranged as pews to listen to the missionary's sermon. In the evening and next morning we listened to the sound of gulls and oyster catchers, soaking in the wild ambience of the island.

We were getting the hang of the changeable weather in Scotland and so it was not a great surprise that more weather fronts were on their way bringing heavy rain and stronger winds for the weekend. We decided to re-track slightly to make for Portree, the main town and capital of Skye, as we needed provisions, and a civilisation fix! We motored the eight or so miles to Portree in complete calm, taking in the sight of groups of guillemots and razorbills, many with a youngster in tow, which we gently steering around. The harbour was spotted with mooring buoys both private and for visitors and was amazingly quiet for the middle of the summer holidays. The town was busier with a good mix of visitors and we discovered the trendy café Arriba as well as The Granary which had excellent, high speed, free Wi-Fi enabling us to download lots of old films to binge watch while the rain hammered down.

Researching local groups who might be interested in the seal campaign I found the Skye Environmental Centre where the International Otter Survival Fund is based. I contacted them and talked to Callum who was very helpful, said he had a personal connection with Norfolk having lived there and promised they would do what they could to support the campaign. He later emailed to say:

> "...this is definitely something we can help you with...I should be able to get a post up on our social media platforms later this week...we have followers from all over the world so it might get to some previously unreached areas!... I've passed it on to Ben our Education Officer and he thinks it would be a great thing to get the kids involved in... they've recently fundraised for 'TeamSeas' which is a big group committed to removing plastic from the oceans."

I contacted Jane, at Friends of Horsey Seals, and she kindly sent photos and a description to Callum which he posted on their social media platform.

*

Contacting groups with a remit and concern for marine wildlife has helped to spread the message of the campaign. Great Yarmouth Sealife kindly gave us the opportunity to commission a display, about the campaign and how to view seals safely, for their native species section. Frisbee, the first seal rescued by the FoHS rescue team, gave an iconic and haunting image of the effects of a plastic flying ring on a seal. She had been brought to East Winch Wildlife Centre in September 2017 starving and weak from her injuries and not able to extend her neck to catch her food. The wounds caused by the ring were the worst the centre manager had seen in 30 years of working with seals. It had been difficult to decide whether it would be kindest to euthanase her that evening. In the event it was agreed to try and treat her.

Display for Sealife, Great Yarmouth

After the yellow ring was cut off Frisbee's neck she lay on her back in her shallow salt bath, perhaps because this was more comfortable for her, and didn't eat for three days. Then, she must have thought, 'I feel a little better now' because she took her first fish. She had a slow, gradual recovery progressing to a deeper, outside pool where we threw fish a distance away from her to encourage her to extend her neck. She was successfully released back onto her beach in February 2018 with a huge wedge scar on her neck but fit and healthy again after five months in care.

Pinkafo had been the second seal rescued by FoHS. I'm glad to say she also recovered and was released bright and healthy on May 1st 2019, after four and a half months of treatment.

Sir David, who weighed only 125 kg when he was rescued, also recovered after being given a similar course of treatment and rehabilitation as Frisbee and Pinkafo. He was released on July 3rd 2019 weighing 200 kg.

A fourth adult grey seal was caught by the FoHS rescue team almost two years later in April 2021. She had been monitored for a very long time during which time her flesh had grown over the plastic ring embedded deep into her neck. She was nicknamed Mrs Vicar because of her white collar. She too was, amazingly, treated and successfully rehabilitated by the highly skilled and dedicated team at RSPCA East Winch Wildlife Centre and was released in July of the same year. (Mrs Vicar is the seal on the top right hand side of the Sealife display).

These four seals have been extremely lucky to survive their ordeal; sadly many others remain entangled in flying rings in the wild.

*

The weather swept through Portree and we hunkered down on Spirit boat-bound for a day as it was too choppy to risk the ride ashore. We stayed longer than planned as the wind turned to a northerly, the direction we were heading, and we finally broke free on Tuesday July 26th to make for Loch Snizort on the north east coast of Skye, our jumping off point for the Outer Hebrides. Dramatic cliffs rise from the sea on the east coast of Skye and we saw the jagged spires of the Old Man of Storr as we motored up in rain and little wind. The forecast northwest breeze didn't materialise until we were approaching the headland and after a short time sailing it turned to a westerly, right on our nose as we passed through the recommended route around the headland of Rubha na h-Aiseig. We then enjoyed a lovely sail with the westerly wind turning fair on our beam, through Loch Snizort and into Loch Greshornish at the southern end. This loch is hospitable for boats with low lying countryside and trees on a gentle slope blanketing the wind. We set the anchor just beyond the few working moorings and spent a peaceful, quiet night there.

Arising early the following morning at 5.30am, the head of the loch was cloaked in mist and the rain pattered down, but by the time we were up and ready to leave all was clear and we motored out and up the loch passing the Ascrib Islands to starboard, heading west towards North Uist in the Outer Hebrides. We had decided to cross to the Outer Hebrides and then start to head south making our way to the Caledonian Canal. Time was beginning to close in and with the weather being unsettled in Scotland with gales following gales we feared the weather windows required to take the northern route via the Orkneys would not materialise.

Our crossing to Loch Maddy in North Uist was very calm with just a little wind to assist our engine and cross the infamous Minch, a normally turbulent stretch of water famous for nasty sea conditions and prolific wildlife including whales, basking sharks and orcas. We saw porpoises and a pod of dolphins at a distance and many groups of guillemots and razorbills, again often with their young, also puffins in ones and twos probably coming from the Shiant Islands further north. The visibility was very good (great for whale watching though we saw none) and we could see the mountains of South Harris compared to the lower lying Uists with their occasional hill. There are a couple of anchorages in Loch Maddy but we were making for the tiny marina, just a couple of pontoons really next to the CalMac ferry terminal, as yet more weather fronts with strong winds and rain were due to arrive over the weekend. Berths are on a first come first served basis and we hoped there would be space. As we approached we could see some fair sized commercial boats on the pontoons but happily there was a gap inside the hammerhead and Richard deftly helmed Spirit into the berth; what a relief.

Loch Maddy marina is a community venture run by an enthusiastic and extremely helpful trust of volunteers one of whom, Edan, greeted us with his friendly dog Spot, a very large boxer-mastiff type cross who, we joked, must be the marina's security. Edan apologised for the noisy ferry terminal work being carried out with diggers and JCBs, gave us the code for the makeshift facilities (all to be redone when the work is completed), and explained where the museum-café and shop were, all within a stone's throw. The museum-café with its integral post office, was a gem and despite the small size of the village the café was practically full. We later realised this museum was one of the main visitor attractions on the island and Loch Maddy the most populated area! Before we collapsed for a snooze I spent some time trying to locate a phone signal, there being none in the marina, to ring Bike Uist to try and secure bicycles for the following day, electric if possible. Amazingly, the answer was 'Yes' and they would be delivered to us at the museum the next morning.

Thursday July 28th was the only day to explore North Uist as the weather was set to be fair, even sunny and warm. Excitedly, we prepared – I even packed my swimming costume, as we had discovered that the Uists are famed for their white sandy beaches. In the museum café, catching up on messages and e-mails, I found that the seal campaign feature had been aired on BBC Look East, 'well done' messages were coming in. The feature also appeared on the BBC webpage on July 28th 2022 with the heading 'Seal supporter sails round Britain for flying rings awareness'. This was fantastic coverage for the campaign and I was hugely grateful to BBC Look East.

We found Guy, who runs Bike Uist, in the car park with two magnificent ex-post office bikes ready to take us on our cycle adventure. He apologised that the electric bikes had not been returned as promised, but he was happy to pick us up from wherever we got to. This would make up for the additional physical exertion we faced!

We cycled from Loch Maddy towards Solas on a quiet, mainly single-track road, then took the right turn towards Clachan sands and finally continued up to the Island of Berneray where the ferry plies to South Harris. We loved the atmosphere and scenery of the parts of the island we saw: its gentle hills rising from the low areas peppered with inland lagoons. We felt the remoteness of an Outer Hebridean island with a small, scattered community who look out for each other. Photographing a renovated thatched croft, we struck up conversation with the chap in the neighbouring house who explained his son had refurbished the croft as a holiday let. We noticed peat had been cut in a nearby area and he said this is still done for burning in the houses though some islanders are against it for environmental reasons. He further explained that the cut peat is stacked in piles in the fields and air dried, normally ready to burn in a month. However, there had been so much rain this summer it had taken much longer. It was an eye opener to see this tradition still being carried on.

Continuing up to Clachan on the western side of the island, open to the Atlantic, we took the winding track to the beach. Arriving through the dunes and onto the machair – grass covered with wildflowers that forms a backdrop to the beaches – we looked out on a vista that could have been the Isles of Scilly or a Caribbean bay. Lit by the sun, the sea displayed a palette of colours from light to deep turquoise through dark blue, bays of white sand stretched far in the low tide to the water's edge and little islands rose up here and there off the shore – stunning. There were a few others there, some with their camper vans, but when we paddled and walked away along the beach we enjoyed solitude.

The amazing Clachan Sands, North Uist

We continued our cycle up the single-track road towards Berneray, saw a pair of swans and their cygnets in one of the dark, peaty lagoons and then crossed the causeway to

Berneray Island. Bike Uist owner Guy, had told us of the café on Berneray (one of the few on the island) and there it was, another little gem with locally baked cakes, artwork, a deck looking out to the sea and a few other cyclists enjoying a drink and a rest. We were on the Hebridean bike trail running some 185 miles from Barra up to the Butt of Lewis.

We were coming to the end of our cycle adventure – unused to cycling far, we could feel our legs (and bottoms) and the post office bikes were great but not lightweight. There was no phone signal at the café to contact Guy to fetch us so we went a little further on to a tiny commercial/fishing harbour and happily found one there, he reassured us he would pick us up in half an hour or so.

At the harbour we chatted to a local man who was tending to a cheerfully painted skiff. He told us the boat was a community venture, built over winter in a nissen hut with few comforts (no electricity or heating). It took four oars plus a coxswain and the group practise rowing it in the bay on their own as there was no one else to race against. There were skiff rallies and competitions elsewhere so we wished him and the group luck in finding a friendly adversary. A Hebridean trail cyclist also paused and said 'Hi', he explained it was the first time he had undertaken such a challenge and he was glad to be doing it.

Guy duly arrived in his truck and loaded the bikes and us for the return journey. On the way back to the marina he told us he had bought a croft with 35 acres five years ago and he loves island life. The cycle-hire business grew from him purchasing bicycles from Cycle of Good Charity, a project which renovates old post office bikes. For each one sold, the project donates a bicycle which is sent to Malawi to assist the local people there: transport gives them better opportunities to start a trade or find work. He also told us of some of the challenges that face the islanders: limited job opportunities, older people who were especially vulnerable during the covid pandemic, and his views on salmon farming. He was not happy with the polluted conditions fish are kept in, nor the way they are taken out of their natural, complex, life cycle. He said the jobs provided by the fish farms were not that many nor pleasant.

We were so glad to have explored some of North Uist on a fair day as on Friday the poor weather arrived as promised. The wind picked up in the afternoon and evening to a gale force 8 (39-46 mph) and rain lashed down. We had been checking when the CalMac ferry was due from Uig on Skye as it berths right next to the marina pontoons and is a mainstay for the island providing a transport link and provisions. We were surprised that it was on its way, if late, given the weather and then even more surprised when it came in and went right out again without berthing! This confused us, was the weather just too bad for it to dock? And if so, would the shop be without bread for us to buy in the morning!? We turned our chart plotter on to track the ferry's position and saw it setting off across the Minch then turning to, apparently, come in again. It took some time but eventually returned and this time docked successfully, phew for us, the crew and the poor passengers. We had noticed the lights of a barge, being used by the construction workers, off the ferry pier and sure enough when I went to buy bread in the morning the shop keeper said this had been in the ferry's way preventing it from docking.

We had secured Spirit with extra lines and after fitting our wooden washboards we relaxed then slept well, snug on our inside berth, as the waves lapped and the wind howled through the rigging.

11

Whales!
and The Christmas Cake Passage

JULY 31ST, 2022

On Sunday July 31st we enjoyed a calm crossing from Loch Maddy to Canna, one of the Small Isles, beginning our journey towards the start of the Caledonian Canal. Surprisingly, given the strong winds of the previous two days, the breeze was so light we were unable to sail and had to resort to motoring. It was another perfect day for spotting whales and dolphins, although we had no expectations as we had seen no sign of either on our first crossing of the Minch. In this vast area we would be very lucky if our tracks happened to cross, especially that of a whale. We had our binoculars out though and Richard was scanning the horizons for any signs of movement or water spouts. The first indication he saw was of water, spouting or splashes it was hard to tell at such a distance, we drew no certain conclusion. Then, quite far off we caught a glimpse of a black back slowly breaking the surface, was it a minke whale? We thought probably it was, but could not be certain, partly because we had seen only pictures of them. We continued on, enjoying groups of guillies, razorbills and then flocks of Manx shearwaters. Suddenly, off our starboard beam perhaps 200 metres away another black back surfaced, disappeared, then surfaced again. This time we saw the small fin towards the rear of the back, it was definitely a minke whale! Wow, we had seen a whale for sure, it was slowly swimming along near the surface, then it must have dived, we didn't see it again.

It was hard to tell how long this minke whale was, they are one of the smaller whales but we know adults grow up to 10 metres, a metre shorter than Spirit. Perhaps an hour later we saw two more minkes again off our starboard beam, nearer this time, perhaps 150 metres away, they were moving in the same manner as the first, slowly swimming along and breaking the surface with their black backs before disappearing. The rules with whales are to maintain course and speed, unless on a collision course when you obviously must give way and it is illegal to be within 100 metres of one, they are highly protected mammals. We abided by this and kept our course whilst I reported our sightings to the Hebridean Whale and Dolphin Trust on their app that I had downloaded earlier. This was a truly amazing, exhilarating experience for us.

As we approached the west coast of Skye we noticed a large group of sea birds circling low and landing, also several splashes. Sea birds are attracted by whales and dolphins feeding, as they can partake of the bounty. Through the binoculars we could see it was porpoises or dolphins making the splashes; we thought they were disorientating and corralling fish in order to catch them. As we continued south nearing Canna, another pod of dolphins way off on our port bow evidently saw us as they rushed towards us and 'played', swimming with our bow wave and diving under Spirit for a short time before moving on. We were relieved it was nothing bigger! The abundance of wildlife we were enjoying surely attested to the good condition of the habitats, the relatively few visitors and associated lack of human disturbance – a welcome by-product of the extreme weather.

In Canna, we spent the night in the main natural harbour, a convenient stopping place coming to and from the Outer Hebrides. There are nine moorings there, operated by the National Trust for Scotland and we were only the third boat in. By late evening all the moorings were taken and another boat was forced to anchor. We spent a quiet evening moored at this wild and special island.

Canna belonged to the Benedictine Monastery of Iona prior to Norway being given sovereignty of the Hebrides in 1098, though the monks continued to live there and cultivate it up to the Reformation. In 1266, it became part of the Kingdom of Scotland. Fast tracking to 1938, the island was sold to a sympathetic purchaser, the Gaelic scholar Dr John Lorne Campbell. In Canna House, he collected the world's largest library of Celtic language and literature and also worked to keep a viable community there. In 1981 he gave the island to the National Trust for Scotland, together with his collections. People still come to visit the library and study on the island.

On Monday August 1st, we needed to complete our passage back from the Outer Hebrides to Tobermory on Mull as weather fronts were forecast, covering most of the UK this time. Strong winds, fog and rain were due to set in from Monday afternoon: we had the morning to get into shelter past the headland of Ardnamurchan Point. The morning winds were forecast to blow from the southwest then south through to southeast force 3-5. Ardnamurchan lies southeast from Canna so we were hoping that we would have the southwesterly wind to give us a fair angle for a straight course before it backed. In addition, there was the concern about wind over tide. It's laborious to make way against the tide, depending on its strength, if there is tide going against a strong wind, a nasty, steep sea is kicked up which is a real slog to cope with. I knew that the Hebridean sea, where we were, is described as twice as rough as the Minch, due to its very uneven seabed, all factors designed to give me some anxiety!

We pushed the tide to make an earlier start aiming to reach Ardnamurchan Point by 1pm, five hours for a 25 mile passage. The tide was not too strong to start with but the southwesterly wind was on the nose through the Sound of Canna forcing us to motor. We were not too worried about this as we would be able to turn once through. However, as we were rounding Rum the wind backed south, straight into us and picked up to Force 4 going on 5. We reefed both our sails and started to tack towards the Point. Wave height increased as the tide turned in our favour, but for the most part Spirit ploughed through as the waves came at an angle on our bow. We took just one big wave in the cockpit as it broke over the spray hood and poured onto me at the helm like buckets of water! At midday, we were eight miles as the crow flies off Ardnamurchan, four hours later we were nearing Tobermory; the passage had taken us over eight hours! I helmed most of the way, mainly to prevent the chance of sea sickness, but also because I enjoy it and it gives a focus, something to do, I certainly was not bored. Richard helmed us into Tobermory and as he did, rain misted in from behind us and the heavens opened, the front had arrived. We were truly grateful for a rain-free passage across the Hebridean Sea with good visibility.

Hard on the wind to Ardnamurchan

Reaching Tobermory we knew it would be busy as it is possibly the most popular harbour on Scotland's West Coast and provides a safe haven in rough weather. We had the advantage of prior knowledge of the harbour moorings and found two vacant ones apart from the others, just off the town, which most people are unaware of. We picked one up, after carefully checking the depth at low water. At the end of a sail, however tired we were, the boat needed to be tended to: covers put on the mainsail and instruments, lines tidy and secure, hot drinks and a snack prepared. This time Richard called for the last of the delicious Christmas cake, kindly made for our departure back in April by a good friend. It had lasted, amazingly, as we had been saving it for times of most need – it had certainly been a 'Christmas cake passage'! Only then did we collapse, limbs aching from bracing and helming, heating on, to dry our wet clothing, absolutely exhausted.

You might ask and wonder what is the attraction of sailing when it can be such a challenge – tough, uncomfortable and sometimes nerve-racking? One of the answers for us is the amazing sense of utter relief and relaxation we have when such a passage is complete; another is the feeling of wonder and achievement that we have crossed the sea and landed on a distant shore, solely by our own efforts and the power of the wind.

We chilled out in Tobermory until the weather fronts had passed through, then motored down the Sound of Mull in calm weather to stay in Oban's transit marina, enabling us to provision up for the Caledonian Canal. We knew it was going to rain again on this passage and Richard stayed on the helm, becoming absolutely drenched in his summer, not so waterproof, jacket, but at least we only had to dry out one set of clothing in Oban. It had been incredible to hear of the drought further south whilst for us, with the exception of a handful of days, it had rained continuously. After the last few days, Richard said enough is enough, he could not take anymore soakings, we needed to push south down the east coast to hopefully experience some sunshine and warmth.

Checking the weather whilst in Oban, we decided to make our passage to Fort William on Monday August 8th and enter the canal the following day, it was time to book a slot. I had been checking the website and the calendar showed all the dates were available for August. However, when we tried to book I realised I had not been scrolling down the page where availability was shown for each type of licence. When I checked the licence we needed, a one way transit of the Caledonian, for Tuesday 9th August it showed 'All

Sold', panic stations! I checked every day for the week and they were all shown as 'Sold'. I managed to get through to one of the lock keepers and she was very helpful, explaining that if I checked online after 5pm it would most likely show the licence was available for next week: the system is set up to show all future dates are 'Sold', when only the next day has reached its limit, a confusing system. I stayed in a state of semi panic until 5pm when I checked the system again and it showed availability for Tuesday. I booked our slot with a sigh of relief.

Still having the weekend to enjoy in Oban bay we moved across to the marina on Kerrera Island, where I had asked for a gas cylinder for our cooker to be put aside for us and diesel was available. Unfortunately, on arrival we found the fuel pontoon blocked by an ex-fishing boat and there was no gas cylinder available. We ended up staying in the marina for two nights to wait for fuel and eventually sourced, reserved, and paid for a gas cylinder in a hardware shop in Fort Augustus halfway along the Caledonian Canal. It appeared that gas cylinders were in very short supply this year.

On Monday 8th August we enjoyed a fantastic downwind sail from Kerrera, via Loch Linnhe to Fort William as planned. A very light southerly wind was forecast for the whole day and so it was as we passed through the Lynn of Lorne. As we sailed north towards the Corran Narrows, in the main part of Loch Linhe, the wind steadily increased. We had the sails 'goose winged', with the mainsail on one side held in place by a preventer line to stop it gybing, and the genoa on the opposite side. This is one of the trickiest points, or directions, of sailing as you have to work to keep both sails filled with wind, without it sneaking behind the main and risking a gybe, when the boom can crash across the boat. We kept an eagle eye on the cable ferry which was regularly crossing the narrows and luckily it passed over just before we sailed through. With the tide sweeping us on, we were making over 7 knots and, with the wind behind us, it would have been tricky to slow down or turn back. The breeze continued to increase up to 23 knots and we were fairly romping up the Loch, it was time to reduce sail and we furled in the Genoa. By the time we reached the anchorage just north of Fort William the wind was howling and the mist started to close in, we were glad to drop the anchor in the shelter of the north facing little bay opposite the canal entrance.

The following morning we were booked to enter the Caledonian Canal at 9am. I knew that it was shallow off the lock at low water but I thought there would be enough depth at that time. I was wrong. We saw another sailing yacht going in around 8.30am and I radioed the lock to find we were too late to join them as our anchor was still down and the tide was ebbing away. We had to wait another four hours. We finally made our way in with two motor cruisers and slices of Battenburg at the ready to de-stress Richard. He had been preparing for the potential calamities of another canal transit by purchasing three extra fenders and a lot of deep breathing!

A positive feature of the Caledonian Canal is that all the locks are operated by the keepers. Skippers and crew have to manage the lines that hold the boats secure front and aft, as well as manoeuvring their craft into position. During our transit sometimes the lock keepers threw down their own lines and occasionally we used our own, throwing them up to the keepers. The first lock went smoothly and once we were raised up, the lock keeper sorted out our paperwork, together with a facilities key to access toilets and showers along the canal.

We began to get to know the crew of Alice and Octavia, the motor cruisers who were on holiday together and destined to be our working team for the first two days to Fort Augustus. We were somewhat concerned when Alice started to exit the lock without the crew undoing her stern line. The name Alice was familiar – we realised that it was the boat we had heard on the ship's radio making a Pan Pan distress call when we were on passage to Oban a few days previously. Their engines had failed and they were drifting towards land. In the end, the Oban lifeboat towed them to the safety of Dunstaffnage marina. As we got talking in the locks to Alice's skipper and mate they confirmed this, explaining a rope had become entangled in both their propellers and they had only one working engine. They had arranged for an engineer to meet them in Inverness to carry out repairs to their second engine. They added that Octavia had also experienced problems when her propellor had picked up a thick fishing rope, she had happily been repaired. We were beginning to wonder if they were both a bit accident prone.

On the first day we successfully negotiated eleven locks including Neptune's Staircase, a flight of no less than eight. Whilst we had only travelled a handful of miles this was enough exertion and stress for one day so we moored at Banavie and treated ourselves to a delicious pub meal. The clouds parted and the sun came out that evening giving us magnificent views of the north face and summit of Ben Nevis. Day two took us through the rest of the ascending locks and lochs Lochy and Oich. We found Lochy to be quite stark and severe: a long, dark stretch of water flanked by steep mountain sides, whilst Oich was gentler and lower lying, with wooded shores and a little island half way along.

Whilst initially hesitant about sharing locks with the two motor boats, we ended up being happy and grateful for the assistance of Joe, Alice's skipper, for leading us and sorting out the opening of locks and bridges for our team all the way to Fort Augustus. He and his crew, a friend and work mate, turned out to be pilots, flying light aircraft for special operations such as land surveys. They were well-versed in traffic control and took a masterful command of all the necessary communications with the lock keepers, chivvying them up before our arrival to try and get the bridges and locks ready and open for a clear, swift passage.

There was a bit of a scare though in the final lock of the day. Locking down is generally easier than locking up as water flowing out of the lock does not create the same strong turbulence as water flowing in. This means there is little pressure on the lines, so long as they are allowed to extend as the boat descends. We were gradually floating down when we became aware there was a problem with Octavia, her bow was being lifted out of the water! We could not see the lock keeper to shout 'stop the water' to and the next minute Adam, Octavia's skipper rushed below, returned with a rather large knife and cut the bow line. Octavia crashed a few feet down to the water and swerved, luckily

Motoring along the Caledonian Canal, Alice and Octavia ahead

without hitting anything. Joe on Alice threw her a line to make fast. What had happened, we think, is that Adam's young son, who had been helping well with the lines up to then, had tied off the bow line on the forward cleat. When the boat continued to descend the line became bar taught and impossible to undo. It's an understandable mistake to make: when locking up you have to tie off as there is so much pressure from turbulence, but when descending the opposite action is needed, lines must not be locked off.

We were the first to enter this last lock so should have been the first to leave, a good position to be in when looking for an available pontoon berth at Fort Augustus. Happily for the others we were dependent on the lock keeper to throw us our lines whilst they had all slipped theirs. He took his time to do this, leaving us stranded, last in the lock. On reaching Fort Augustus, all the pontoons were full, but we managed to squeeze into a tight space alongside a stone wharf with no shore power.

We planned to have a rest day in Fort Augustus but we knew that without a 240v supply our batteries would be flat within 24 hours and the food in the fridge would then start to deteriorate. In the morning we were up early to spring cat-like into action and grab a space on the main pontoon equipped with shore power and water. Richard spied a yacht leaving but as we loosened our lines a small red, pedal driven trimaran started to head towards it. I ran down to meet them, and begged them to take another space on the inside of the pontoon, which they kindly did.

An unforeseen aspect of transiting the Caledonian Canal is the fact that on a boat you become one of the main visitor attractions, especially at the two main flights of locks. As I handled Spirit's lines from the quaysides a number of people asked questions: 'How much does it cost to travel the Caledonian?', answer £245 for our size boat, 'How long does it take?', 'Where have we come from?, 'Can your boat cross oceans?'. Crowds of visitors of various nationalities: Polish, American, Indian, Israeli, Dutch, French and British had come to visit Scotland and were now watching and taking photos of us and Spirit! I also chatted here and there to some of the lock keepers, one of whom said he had been a warden on the remote island of St Kilda for two years. Whilst I passed the time of day, poor Richard, stranded on the boat, was having to motor Spirit into the locks without incurring any damage, as well as tending the two winches controlling her lines as the water swirled about. He was in no humour to answer any tourist queries.

We decided to spend three of our seven nights' allowance, part of our transit licence, in Fort Augustus. The weather finally turned warm and sunny for us and the village was attractive, with a friendly, personable atmosphere and enough interest, cafés and walks to keep us both happy. The lock flight provided the main event, running through the centre with cafés and pubs on one side, cottages on the other. We collected the gas cylinder we had previously ordered back in Kerrera and stopped at a book sale at one of the cottages. The owner explained he was raising funds for two schools one in Cambodia, the other in Nepal. He had volunteered at both and was hoping to return to the one in Nepal at the end of the year. We were glad to support his noble cause.

The Caledonian Canal Centre in Fort Augustus has a pocket size exhibition giving a wealth of well-presented facts about the building of the canal. We found out it took 18 years to complete, opening in 1822 and was inspired and managed by Thomas Telford who was responsible for most of the major highways and bridges in Scotland, as well as the Menai Straits Suspension Bridge in Wales. The canal is 60 miles long, joining one side of Scotland to the other and many of the workers who built it were subsistence farmers and fishermen who had never earned a wage before.

The canal takes advantage of a major fault line created 428 million years ago when two great tectonic plates collided. The line of the fault was swept clean by glaciers during the Ice Age leaving a huge trench. Telford realised his vision of making a safe passage for trading sailing vessels, which had for years been battling their way around the top of Scotland on a hazardous 300 mile passage. Ironically, during the time the canal was built, steam overtook sail as the primary means of propulsion for merchant ships and the long delays previously encountered by sailing ships were no longer an issue, though the canal still provided a shorter and safer passage.

Preparing Spirit to leave Fort Augustus on a still, misty morning we were bothered by midges, almost for the first time on this trip, and donned our midge head-nets, which helped a lot. We successfully completed the staircase of six locks, recovered ourselves with breakfast in a café and then motored the full length of Loch Ness, all 23 miles, as the morning mist lifted, allowing the sun to shine. There was little wind until it freshened into a northeast breeze, right on our nose forcing us to use the engine.

Loch Ness must be one of the most famous stretches of water in the world. It holds a gigantic 263 billion cubic feet of water which is more than the water of all the lakes, rivers and reservoirs in England and Wales combined! Another claim to fame lies in it providing an extensive habitat for the legendary Loch Ness monster. The earliest report of Nessie, as this sea monster is affectionately known, was recorded by Adomnan in the 6th Century in his account of St Columba. He described how St Columba came across some locals burying a man by the river Ness who they said had been mauled and killed by a sea monster. St Columba sent his companion to swim across the river and as he did so the said beast appeared. St Columba made the sign of the cross and uttered the words 'Go no further, do not touch the man. Go back at once.' The beast stopped 'as if pulled back with ropes' and fled! We had no sighting of Nessie but did have our first, I think, of two ospreys. We had never seen ospreys before but they looked the right shape had light colouring, were definitely large raptors but not eagles. They flapped as they flew quite high right down the loch and we knew that ospreys frequented the area.

We were almost at the end of our Caledonian Canal cruise to Inverness. Whilst canal transits are not Richard's first choice, his stress levels were much lower this time with the locks being bigger than in the Crinan, reducing the risk of collision. Also, he rigged a much better system of line handling, enabling both the bow and stern lines to be controlled from the cockpit, added three extra fenders to protect Spirit and had a number of welcome rest days with no lock handling required. We still had most of a Battenburg cake left!

12

1200 Miles Sailed, 500 To Go!

AUGUST 14TH, 2022

After negotiating the final flight of locks at Muirtown, we spent our last day on the Caledonian Canal at Seaport marina enjoying hot showers and making use of the laundry. We also did a quick explore of Inverness, which is within easy walking distance of the marina. Entering a big town with its myriad of shops and throngs of people always seems a bit overwhelming when sailing, so after a pick-me-up coffee and hot chocolate we found our way to the broad river Ness, that runs through the centre of the town. Pleasant paths run on either side and we found a footbridge to cross over. At the river we were entranced by a group of merganser diving ducks. We had seen them at a distance through binoculars on our wild life days in Mull and here they were, a few metres away, diving down, swimming around searching for food; we could see them clearly through the crystal, shallow water.

We booked our exit of the canal with Emma, one of the lock keepers I had spoken to when I was panicking about all the canal licences being sold out. The next morning saw us making our way through the final section comprising a lock, railway swing bridge, then the final sea lock. That final lock is quite a transition: from the contained waters of the canal you are finally cast out into the sea. We had been in this lock once before and it was not a pleasant experience. About 20 years ago we bought Craigana, a Contessa 32 which is a supremely sea-worthy small yacht and one of the few designs to come through the infamous 1979 Fastnet Race disaster relatively unscathed. This little yacht inspired us with such confidence in poor weather that it led to us eventually buying Spirit, a similar design in a larger form.

After we had bought Craigana in Hartlepool, we sailed her to Inverness with the help of a young Northern Irish delivery skipper, Bron. The trip went well all the way up the North East coast, with good weather despite it being March. Then, we encountered strong head winds on the final leg. With wind against tide, as you now know, the sea was kicked up. Arriving late at Inverness we knew the sea lock was left open overnight and we thought there would be shelter in there, we thought wrong! There was a strong swell into the lock and the waves were sloshing around like the inside of a washing machine: we had committed ourselves into a dead-end. After quickly abandoning the plan of climbing the ladder to secure our lines, Bron had to extricate Craigana backwards between the solid stone walls of the lock. Thinking about it now, did that explain some of Richard's paranoia of taking Spirit into a canal?

This time the sea was calm in both the sea lock and the Moray Firth. We motored just a few miles up the Firth to anchor overnight in Fortrose Bay which sheltered us from the northerly wind. The following day we did another short passage in calm conditions to Cromarty Firth harbour, which had been recommended as a pleasant place to stop, with free visitor mooring buoys. As we made our way up

Seals seen at sea, cormorants in the Moray Firth

the Firth we had sightings of several grey seals bottling, with their snouts lifted upwards. We had seen seals all around the coast during our trip: often individuals had popped up wherever we were sailing, close to land or well offshore; we had seen groups of seals hauled out on rocks; and others frequented the harbours we had visited, drawn by the fishing boats and the spoils they discharged.

Cromarty Firth is a place of extreme contrast: as we passed the attractive wooded headland to port, Nigg Energy Park came into view to starboard. This is a massive facility which services both oil and clean renewable energy production in the North Sea. Three humongous oil rigs were anchored up the middle of the Firth. Compare this with the small, historic village of Cromarty with its attractive old streets and buildings on the opposite banks of the estuary.

Arriving by boat we had little idea of what we were going to find ashore and Cromarty was a delight. The Courthouse was open, with exhibitions and a clever re-enactment of a 19th century trial and we saw the cottage where Hugh Miller, an influential Scotsman, self-taught geologist, folklorist and evangelical Christian, was born in 1802. Being well-visited it had a couple of nice cafés which featured on our 'best spots list' together with shelter, walks and a good phone signal! Finally there was The Cheese House, a unique shop with a big selection of Dutch cheeses and some Scottish.

The leg from Cromarty to Rattray Head runs horizontally east-west and we were on the lookout for suitable winds to blow us eastwards. With land to the south a southerly or southwest wind coming off the land, thus promising a flat sea, would be ideal. The forecast was for east going southeast then veering south-southwest for the next couple of days. We had a blow from the east the evening before departure then the wind did veer as forecasted, allowing us to sail in fair winds past the bay of Findhorn, home of the fabled spiritual, eco-based community, and on towards Lossiemouth.

On the trip I mentioned with Craigana, Lossiemouth was the final harbour we stopped at before Inverness and it was a nostalgic return for us. It was much how we remembered it – a small marina nestled into the traditional stone walls of a fishing harbour with an entrance that was not easy to negotiate. We missed the visitor berths and found one space amongst the local boats where the friendly harbourmaster allowed us to stay put. The trip long ago with Craigana gave us a taste of what it would be like to leave a home base and keep going, a bit akin to undertaking a long distance hiking trail rather than a circular walk. We loved the feeling of carrying on then and now we had the good fortune to be doing this over an extended period of time.

Richard had been keeping contact with Colin, (who we last saw in Dale, Milford Haven), over the summer, following his progress ahead of us through the Caledonian Canal. Colin had received the offer of a two-week holiday in Spain versus continuing his voyage around Scotland. It was a no-brainer! He decided to leave Bella Vela in a Scottish harbour over winter and resume his round Britain trip the following year. We knew that Bella Vela was moored in Lossiemouth and had assured Colin we would look out for her if we stopped there. We found her safe and secure in one of the permanent marina berths and sent a photo to Colin to reassure him all was well.

The southwesterly wind continued the next day and we had an exhilarating sail to Whitehills, another even smaller, former fishing harbour. The day started sunny and calm and gradually the wind picked up to southwest force 4-5 (13-24 mph). We were making 7 knots, even glimpsing a couple of 8s, a great speed for a medium sized yacht. I had researched Whitehills' harbour entrance, read the sailing directions and seen a video of someone entering. It looked very tricky and I had discounted it at first, but then we had heard it was a friendly, community harbour and manageable to enter in calm seas. I had not actually shown Richard the video though, I knew he would be helming and I had not wanted to scare him!

Bertie, the harbourmaster, was not answering when I tried to call up on our approach, but someone was on the harbour wall who turned out to be the harbourmaster's assistant, he kindly directed us to the deeper water in the short, narrow approach channel. The tide was falling and it was nearing low water. There was no sign of the harbour entrance in the channel, just a ramp straight ahead, part of the old lifeboat station. It was not dissimilar to the clashing rocks challenge in the Voyage of Sinbad. Complete faith was needed in the sailing directions – only when we were fully committed were we rewarded with the appearance of the hidden entrance to port. Richard pushed the helm hard over, the sea gods stayed with us and we were safely in.

We enjoyed a rest day at Whitehills, watching yachts leaving the harbour to race in the morning, before taking the bus to Portsoy, the next village, which became the island of Todday in the 2016 re-make of the 1949 film Whisky Galore. We were keen to see the village as we had downloaded the

The narrow entrance to Whitehills to left of photo

film and had thoroughly enjoyed watching it. Eddie Izzard stars as the bumbling Captain Waggett whom the villagers run rings around. The film crew were in the village for about two months and apparently created a real buzz, with many of the locals acting as extras. Portsoy was also the set for the Canadian village in the TV series Peaky Blinders.

On Sunday August 21st, we could not miss the advantage of a southwesterly wind blowing off the land and were up at 5am to head towards Peterhead around the corner and south from the Moray Firth. To reach it we had to pass Rattray Head, where the tides run hard and a shallow area can kick up a turbulent sea in adverse conditions. Hence our early start: to go with the tide and reach the Head before it turned against us. We just made it and the conditions were fairly calm. A mile off the harbour breakwaters of Peterhead we radioed Port Control and they gave us permission to enter this busy commercial harbour and head towards the little marina. Our passage had taken six and a half hours at an average speed of 6.3 knots and a top speed of 8.3 knots, with help from the tide. We had sailed all the way.

We were fairly whacked and quite happy to find the weather, with fronts and a southerly wind forecast, was suggesting we have a few days off in the unlikely tourist stop of Peterhead.

We ended up being wind-bound in Peterhead for a week due to strong southerlies and a couple of fronts bearing rain and mist. In between, the sun did shine and we were able to explore. Our first trek took us along the perimeter of the outer harbour, through part of the town to the fish quays and the Dolphin café, next to the Port Authority offices. From the safety of the café, frequented by the local fishermen, we looked out onto the fleet of berthed trawlers, discharging their catch and replenishing with diesel and water, ready to head back out to sea. The sight of the exposed machinery and steel cables adorning the decks of these huge vessels was truly terrifying. How people can safely operate this equipment whilst being tossed around on the open ocean was beyond our comprehension. When we later asked the harbourmaster how sustainable the fishing was, he explained about quotas and added that 90% of these are held by just four Scottish fishing families operating out of Peterhead and nearby Fraserburgh.

Peterhead is a major port for big fishing boats and ships servicing offshore energy installations. It's the only large, safe harbour on this unforgiving, exposed stretch of

Scottish coast. The two long breakwaters that render it a secure haven took 70 years to complete and are inextricably linked to Peterhead Prison. During the 19th century public demand for a 'Harbour of Refuge' grew in the face of so many shipwrecks on this coast and the huge engineering project was agreed through an Act of Parliament. Peterhead, a convict prison which took men sentenced to hard labour, was opened in 1888 to provide a cheap workforce. The prisoners were transported in secure railway carriages to the nearby Stirling Hill quarry, where they broke up the local pink granite rock with sledgehammers for the foundations of the breakwaters.

After 125 years and a chequered history of over-crowding, poor conditions, rioting and bravery of prison warders, as well as the accomplishment of building the harbour breakwaters, the prison gates were closed to offenders and the replacement prison HMP Grampian was built next door. The gates of the old prison were reopened in 2016 as a museum and visitors are welcomed to peek into the murky depths of both prisoners' and prison warders' experience. Recommended highly by Keith, the friendly harbourmaster, we too entered through Admiralty Gate to don audio headphones and immerse ourselves into a world apart.

The prison museum was very well presented with friendly staff dressed in prison warder uniform at the start and end. Some of them used to work at the prison. Visitors are able to wander where they wish following an audio trail, which gives descriptions and actual voices of warders relating stories and traumas of everyday prison life. Seeing footage of some of our older prisons on TV, for example on the news and episodes of the serial Porridge, did not prepare us for the bleak, stark reality of life inside. The frequent feeling of tension arising from the interactions between some prisoners and warders was palpable. This sometimes arose during the degrading routine of slopping out or at communal meal times. We were grateful to enjoy a break in the cheery, modern café with equally cheerful staff before completing our tour and escaping!

On our way out we visited the special RNLI exhibition room housing the beautifully renovated lifeboat, the Julia Park Barry of Glasgow, named after her benefactor. This lifeboat was actually on station in Peterhead and in 1940 was involved in the dramatic rescue of crews of some four ships that ran aground in a storm on the infamous Rattray Head, all on the same day! This was the same Rattray Head we rounded on our way to Peterhead. This lifeboat was in service from 1939 to 1969 and saved 496 lives during this time.

Back in the marina, relaxing in Spirit's saloon, we sometimes became aware of voices outside. Looking out, we realised these came from cold water swimmers. With, but more often without wetsuits, some enjoyed their sport in small groups and combined it with a social chat! Amazingly there was a five-star sandy beach just across from the marina in this harbour within a harbour. The stars attest to good bathing water quality and a little caravan site, playground and water sports centre have all grown up around the beach. I eventually built up the courage to swim on our last day, wetsuit-less. It was cold and exhilarating, my skin felt as if it was burning!

At last the wind changed to a favourable direction and the weather improved with high pressure building across the UK. It was time to leave and continue our journey south. We actually felt sad to leave Peterhead. Whilst the town presents as a bit plain and bleak, the marina was fine and cheap at £20 per night, with harbourmasters who proved helpful, friendly and informative. We had also discovered some unlikely Peterhead gems.

13

Another Whale! and Southbound

AUGUST 26TH, 2022

For the next few days we hopped from one harbour to the next; the coast line is fairly straight with few indentations and virtually nowhere to anchor. We set off from Peterhead in calm, windless conditions motoring along an almost smooth, glassy sea. A few miles south, before reaching the wind farm off Aberdeen, we came across literally hundreds of sea birds rafting out on the water. They just seemed to be resting and chilling out, with a few more concentrated groups possibly feeding. There were gulls, guillemots and many razorbills with lots of young ones, now well fledged. The wind then picked up from the southeast and we were able to sail on our southwest course to the attractive harbour of Stonehaven where we had arranged with the harbourmaster to berth alongside the harbour wall.

It was nearing springs, which meant a large rise and fall in the tide, and with no pontoon to take Spirit up and down with the water, we rigged up a complicated arrangement of long lines, complete with buckets of water to keep her under control. As the lines securing the boat have to be very long, to cater for the rise and fall of tide, there is a tendency for the boat to drift some distance away from the wall. Hanging two buckets filled with water, on the bow and stern lines, exerts a downwards pull, snugging the boat up to the wall. We enjoyed the rest of the day exploring the attractive town of Stonehaven; sitting in the sun on the upstairs balcony of a harbour-side café and walking along the boardwalk to the Art Deco lido set back from the beach.

Our next port was Arbroath, another traditional harbour just 30 miles on and famous for its Arbroath Smokies, fillets of smoked haddock. This time we needed to arrive whilst the tide was up and the lock gates to the inner harbour, now a little marina, open. On our passage we had very light following winds and decided to try every means possible to sail rather than run the engine: first, we hoisted our main sail with its preventer line but were making little headway; second, we hoisted the cruising chute with the mainsail but the chute would not fill as it was blanketed by the mainsail; third, we lowered the mainsail to try the chute on its own, still little speed; fourth, we dropped the chute and goose-winged our main and genoa, poling the genoa out, still no headway; fifth, everything down and we stuck the engine on! At least these manoeuvres kept us both busy and entertained.

High tide allowed us through the lock gates and into Arbroath harbour without mishap. It constantly amazes us how boats of all sizes and weights are carried into these locked-in harbours by the rising water, which then disappears in the approach channels to practically nothing!

Next day, governed by the tide and opening of the lock gates, the earliest we could leave was shortly after midday. We decided to head for the River Tay, to break our passage to Eyemouth, rather than risk arriving at its tricky harbour entrance after dark. The River Tay has strong tides flooding in and out and we knew we had the flood to carry us the eight miles upriver, where we had heard the Royal Tay Yacht Club provided a free mooring buoy off the town of Broughty Ferry. It's possible to anchor there as well, but the seabed is reported to be 'foul' with mooring tackle. We were keen to locate the buoy and hoped it would be free, as I had not been able to make contact with the club over the past few days to check.

It was a beautiful, warm, sunny afternoon as we motored the six miles down to the entrance of the Tay and then up to the moorings. I rang the yacht club one last time and miraculously they answered. I explained we were visiting from the Royal Cinque Ports Yacht Club and a friendly voice reassured us we were heading straight for the buoy and were welcome to use it. We attached Spirit to the mooring and relaxed in the knowledge that the racing tides would not sweep us up to Dundee or out to sea!

When we are on passage we deflate our dinghy and secure it on deck away from the sails and working areas of the boat. During a short stop such as this one, we stay on board as it takes some time and effort to deploy the dinghy and then get it on board again. This gives 'permission' to do whatever jobs are needed then relax on board, eat and get an early night, ready for sailing the next day.

The entrance to the River Tay lies east-west and whilst we only had light easterly winds we could only leave on the ebb which meant some wind over tide and quite a choppy ride to exit the river. As we bore off the wind to head south, leaving the river behind us, the sea flattened. In fact, there was so little wind we motored across the Firth of Forth in calm seas. We were abeam of the Isle of May which lies in the middle of the firth when we saw a black back breaking the surface of the water. In split seconds we both thought, 'is it a dolphin?' then, as the back continued and continued to rise, I exclaimed, 'my goodness it's big – it's a minke!' It was perhaps 100 or so metres away. We had not realised there are minkes on the north east coast and were so pleased to see it and be able to identify it from our previous sightings on the west coast. Quite a few miles further on, still in the firth we had a fantastic sighting of a second minke. This one was travelling towards us, on our starboard side, surfacing up and down a couple of times in the water. As it came near and surfaced again Richard saw water pouring from its mouth, we guess from feeding, amazing! We were taken by surprise to see another whale and although it was not moving very fast I did not have time to grab and focus my camera to take a picture.

Reaching the south side of the Firth of Forth we were passing St Abbs Head when the swell picked up, making for an interesting approach to Eyemouth harbour which is flanked by rocks. There is a blind turn into the harbour which is quite busy with fishing vessels and now 'wind cats' (short for windfarm servicing large motor catamarans), so we followed the protocol and radioed to get the OK to proceed from the harbourmaster. This was another nostalgic return as we were last in Eyemouth on our voyage with Craigana. The harbour was similar to how we remembered it: traditional stone built docks and resident seals mooching around looking for food. Gulls gather for fish scraps as well when the fishing boats flush their bilges. Sadly, it was a bit dirty with diesel and litter. The harbourmaster was very pleasant, directing us to the visitor pontoon which had been added since we were last there. I did mention the diesel and he was aware and responsive.

We had just one night in Eyemouth, leaving before low tide the next morning, to avoid grounding off the shallow pontoon. The wind was coming from the northeast, exactly the direction of the departure line from the entrance so this time the swell was against us making it a lumpy ride to get out. In a stronger wind from this direction the harbour would be untenable. We radioed our intentions to depart and followed a small fishing boat out, a larger one was standing by to let us both pass and they returned our wave of thanks.

We had plenty of time to reach Holy Isle, also known as Lindisfarne, and the Farne Islands as the tide runs fast through the islands and was not turning south until 2pm. Hoisting our main sail only, we wafted southwards at around 3 knots running against the tide. Eight miles on we were passing Berwick upon Tweed and crossing the border into England, time to lower our Scottish courtesy flag after our two and a half month visit. The tide was turning as we sailed downwind abreast of Holy Island. We had thought about anchoring in the harbour at Lindisfarne but at springs it can be tricky and a bit shallow so we continued on to Amble. There were a few puffins still about, they migrate north in August, and a number of razorbills but we knew that the islands had unfortunately sustained huge losses from bird flu this year.

Amble marina is tucked in a basin just up the River Coquet, with a cill that retains the water as the tide ebbs out, we arrived on high water with plenty of depth to get in. We were very impressed with the marina: it's clean and very well organised with a visitor pack on the reception pontoon containing a gate pass, information and a plan of the pontoons naming all the boats which included Spirit! They also offered a discount for a week's stay and with time to spare, as we were not due at Fosdyke until the end of September, we decided to make use of it. An added bonus was the variety of bird life in the marina and on the river: we heard the gentle splashes of diving eider ducks and the bigger splash of a cormorant fishing; goosanders regularly frequented the marina and we saw herons, egrets, redshanks, cormorants, swans and a variety of gulls up the river with skeins of brent geese flying overhead morning and evening.

Having recovered from our 10 hour passage from Eyemouth with a similar length sleep, we explored ashore next morning and treated ourselves to breakfast in 1911, the café recommended by the marina staff. A walk upstream along the river Coquet took us to the attractive village of Warkworth with its medieval castle, church and hermitage. The following day we took the bus, enjoying a roller coaster ride, right at the front of the top deck to Barter Books in Alnwick .

Barter Books is an amazing second-hand book shop based in the impressive disused railway station at Alnwick. The station itself was built in 1887 in grand style to impress royal visitors to Alnwick Castle. Trains ran until the infamous Beeching cuts in 1968 and there is hope they may one day run again, due to the restoration efforts of the volunteers of the Aln Valley Railway. Mary Manley, with the support of her husband Stuart, decided to open a second-hand bookshop in 1991 on the swap system and call it 'Barter Books'. This has developed not only into one of the largest second-hand book shops in Britain, but also a wholly immersive literary experience. The shop houses over 350,000 books and is beautifully organised into over 70 sections. A model railway, running at ceiling level, provides a spirit of the past and perhaps the future; a café with tables in the original station waiting rooms, beautifully furnished and warmed by open fires in winter, offers sustenance; three large murals and numerous quotes inspire; and Victorian conversation chairs provide comfy seats to relax and read in. We left with our choices: Richard bearing the riveting reads of Skeene's 'Elements of Yacht Design' and 'Repairing Long Case Clock Cases' as well as a rare leap into fiction, with 'Norwegian Wood' by Haruki Murakami; and I chose 'A Quiet Life' by Beryl Bainbridge and 'The Little Coffee Shop of Kabul' by Deborah Rodriguez.

The amazing Barter Books in Alnwick

We enjoyed a few days of warmth and sun in Amble, which is a down-to-earth sort of town, with a bustling high street and working harbour area. It used to be a busy port of trade with emissaries from Europe based there, now there is some re-development with retail pods, seafood cafés and apartments looking over the marina.

On Friday morning we took advantage of the sunshine and completed a deck painting job then jumped on the roller coaster bus again to visit Alnmouth. This is a very pretty village on the mouth of the River Aln, with one of Northumberland's stunning sandy beaches stretching in both directions. We paddled and I swam in shallow breakers. Looking out to sea I glimpsed a very slim black shape which appeared to be swimming within the side of a wave, then it disappeared. I was slightly worried: was it a child in a wetsuit? I kept looking and then saw it was actually a cormorant! It was quite amazing to see it swimming, side on, through the translucent wall of water. We wandered back through the village and shared a wood-fired pizza in a very cosy, unspoilt pub, complete with lounging labradors and their friendly, chatty humans.

The week's stay in Amble provided an ideal opportunity to change the oil in our inboard diesel engine. This should ideally be changed every 100 hours and definitely before the boat is lifted ashore for the winter. This had been preying on Richard's mind as we closed towards Fosdyke where Spirit would be lifted out of the water as soon as we arrived. We were able to order the right oil and filters from the engine manufacturer and have them delivered to the marina at Amble. Running up the engine to warm the oil Richard was then able to change both it and the filter, disposing of the old ones at the collection station provided by the marina. Another necessary job completed.

I was continuing to promote the seal campaign by talking to shops in Amble and asking them if they would sell solid frisbees rather than flying rings to protect the seals. I visited two shops: both owners listened and took a leaflet. The first said: 'I haven't many rings left...', but the woman in the second, one of the retail pods near the harbour selling pet items, was very receptive and took her dog play rings off display immediately! She said she always cuts rings open, such as plastic pull rings, to protect birds getting caught in them, but she didn't know about the danger to seals from flying rings. In Alnmouth, I spoke to the owner of the Post Office cum local shop who was also selling beach toys. He said he did have flying rings for sale but he listened, took a leaflet and appeared receptive.

*

The generic term flying ring covers all types of throwing rings: the danger to seals being the hole in the middle. The first seal I had heard of getting entangled in a flying ring, was a grey bull seal which was spotted on the beach at Ravenscar, North Yorkshire, with a dog toy ring around his neck. He was captured by an RSPCA team with the help of Scarborough Sealife Sanctuary. The ring was cut off and thankfully the seal released on August 25th 2017.

*

Before our week in Amble was up we had a welcome visit from two friends. Hilary and Nigel drove all the way up from King's Lynn for a two day visit, bearing the gift of a huge apple cake to replenish our passage-cake supply. It was very exciting to see their familiar, friendly faces and we enjoyed time together in this lovely Northumberland setting catching up, as we took a long beach and river walk also re-visiting Barter Books. They treated us to our first evening meal out in six months at their comfortable, spacious hotel. Their journey back took several hours; ours would take two weeks.

14

Whitby –
In the Wake of Dracula's Ship Demeter!

SEPTEMBER 6TH, 2022

Our week in Amble was up and we left on Tuesday September 6th for Tynmouth, planning to anchor in the outer harbour, before continuing on further south to Hartlepool and then to Whitby. The forecast was not perfect, with light southeasterly winds and rain showers, which meant motoring was likely. As we left Amble there was quite an onshore swell which died down as we turned south, past Coquet Island and some of its resident seals. The sea was then quite calm as we motored south with just our mainsail raised for stability. As we approached Tynemouth however, the wind built up to force 5 touching 6, together with rain and an increasing swell. Thankfully, the entrance to the harbour is wide which gave us plenty of room to surf in on the waves. We reached the relative calm of the anchorage, sheltered by the southern breakwater, as the rain squall turned into a thunderstorm with lightning flashes and thunder breaking overhead, we were drenched! Having dropped our mainsail and sorted ourselves out with rolls and a hot drink we assessed the anchorage. It was rolly, very rolly; the swell was getting into the harbour, rocking Spirit uncomfortably from side to side, so we decided to seek better shelter at the nearest marina and radioed Royal Quays just two miles up the river. There was plenty of space for us and they opened their lock gates as we approached. The heating went on, just as in Scotland, to dry out our clothes.

We took a day off in Tynemouth to let the swell die down and the wind to change from the southeast to the north. In the morning, I took a walk round the marina and found a pilot boat with crew, berthed on the outer pontoon. I asked their advice about local forecasts for wave height and swell and they put me onto Cefas WaveNet Interactive Map, a government website which gives real time readings from buoys moored around the coast. The readings gave some indication of the conditions we could expect when sailing and approaching the exposed entrances of ports on this northeast coast.

We had checked the weather for continuing to Hartlepool: a force 2-4, east-northeast wind and one metre swell, all good for going south. We had not been prepared for mist though! There was a thick fog as we left Tynmouth entrance and the foghorn was booming. We put our navigation lights, radar and AIS systems on and I studied the radar as Richard helmed in no wind and a fairly calm sea, the swell had died down. Poor visibility is one of the most unnerving conditions at sea but the radar and AIS are invaluable, they gave us a good picture of where other vessels were, even though we could not physically see them. As we cleared land, the mist lifted giving us back a welcome view of sea and the coastline in the distance. The wind never picked up so we motored with our main up and reached Hartlepool as planned, within a fair tide and at high water, which we needed to navigate up the shallow entrance channel and into the lock at the marina. This is the marina where we started our delivery trip with Craigana and brought back fond memories. The marina was little changed but the fishermens' café where Richard had enjoyed his morning sausage sandwich when working on the boat back then was gone, replaced with a range of little eateries, some of which still offered hot breakfast rolls.

We learnt that evening, September 8th, of the Queen's passing: there was a strange feeling of loss and the end of an era.

We poured over the weather in Hartlepool as WaveNet was showing an increased northeast swell of 2.2 metres, this was being caused by strong winds up in Scotland travelling down the North Sea. Our next planned stop was Whitby where the entrance is open to the north and the breakwaters are close together: we knew it could be dangerous in strong northerly winds and swell. The Sailing Directions emphasised this, 'In strong onshore winds...the whole of this area becomes impossible with considerable broken water. "Having a look" is not an option.'

We were not able to leave Hartlepool until 1pm because of the late high water so I rang Whitby harbour twice that morning to check the conditions. Both times the swell in the entrance was reported to be only one metre and the conditions OK. A north-northeast wind was forecast building to force 5 in the evening. We reckoned to be in by then and when we checked the swell at sea it had reduced, so we decided to go. Our fall back plan if we could not enter Whitby was to continue on to an anchorage protected from north winds at Filey. This was some way south and we would not be there before dark.

As we left the marina lock gates, quite a big swell was coming into the entrance channel. Richard helmed Spirit carefully and gradually through, as it was shallow, only two and a half metres, and we didn't want our keel to touch the bottom in the troughs. All was well and the depth gradually increased.

The swell continued, but as we turned towards Whitby it was coming from an easier direction on our port quarter. The wind was already a force 4 and we raised the mainsail with two reefs in and then a scrap of genoa for balance and power. This was a good sail in the biggest seas we have encountered all summer: the swell lifted us up then passed underneath. Winds went up to the predicted force 5 but not above. Spirit romped along at between 6 to 7 knots. She took the conditions completely in her stride and passages like this made us grateful for choosing such a classic, sea-worthy design. We had not made it into the safety of Whitby harbour yet though.

As we neared our last waypoint before turning towards Whitby harbour I radioed the harbourmaster again to check conditions at the entrance. He advised that the conditions were poor with confused seas and an estimated swell of two metres. With the harbour entrance in sight we assessed the conditions, conferred, and decided to proceed. As it was, Richard helmed Spirit excellently through the turmoil of water, with waves crashing over the breakwater ledges. We soon reached the calm of the inner harbour and I gave a thumbs-up to the crowd of visitors on the pier taking pictures of us. Many of them returned with waves and cheers, it was a moment of shared humanity and relief. We had landed at Whitby in the wake of the ship Demeter, created by Bram Stoker in his famous novel Dracula!

The narrow Whitby entrance in calmer weather!

Both of us had been so looking forward to a break in Whitby, which was a favourite day trip for Richard as a child and for us both during the many years when Yorkshire was our home. The sailing directions aptly described it:

'Whitby is justifiably popular with visiting yachtsmen, it has the best yachting facilities on the Yorkshire coast and is a very fine town, a major historic attraction, its connection with Captain Cook is well known. Dracula came here as a large dog.'(!)

The harbourmaster came to welcome us, a droll ex-fisherman, he explained some of the history of the harbour and where to visit. I asked if there was anything particular on this weekend and he replied he loses count, as there are that many festivals of folk music, Goth gatherings and

Steam Punks, not to mention the Druids who gather on solstices at the iconic Whitby Abbey.

That evening in search of celebratory sustenance we found the Magpie café and treated ourselves to excellent fish and chips with a delicious veggie alternative for me. We had enjoyed the sail but it had been peppered with some anxiety about getting into Whitby and whether the wind would increase earlier than forecasted, so it was a huge relief to be there. Back aboard, we enjoyed total relaxation and a good, long sleep.

We had a few days to reacquaint ourselves with the delights of Whitby and started by visiting the Captain James Cook museum. The story and exhibits are housed in the home previously owned by John Walker, a merchant ship owner and Quaker, who took young James on as one of his apprentices. Coming from a humble, farming background Cook's rise to becoming one of the most accomplished captains and navigators of the 18th century was unusual. We learnt about the three extraordinary circumnavigations Cook led to chart unknown lands, including the East coast of Australia, New Zealand and the Bering Straits. He took scientists and naturalists with him to illustrate and record their discoveries of native peoples: their culture, flora and fauna. He also sailed to the island of Tahiti in 1761 for them to observe the transit of Venus. This rare celestial alignment was a crucial moment in astronomical history as it enabled astronomers to accurately determine the distance of the earth from the sun and from other planets in our solar system.

Cook appeared to be a strong and fair man who treated the people he met with openness and respect, with few incidents of using force. On meeting the Polynesians he was evidently impressed with their extensive seafaring and navigation skills. He was also known for the care he gave to his crew, stocking up on fresh provisions to keep them healthy and free from scurvy. The ships he chose for the expeditions were coal-carrying Colliers built in Whitby, of which he had previous experience of sailing. He knew them to be very strong, sea-worthy, able to carry large loads and also to take the ground. This last attribute proved invaluable after Endeavour struck the Great Barrier Reef. Cook was able to run the ship aground on the East coast of Australia to save the vessel from sinking and make repairs on the beach, enabling them to continue their voyage to completion.

The fascinating Captain Cook museum, Whitby

Whilst in Whitby we enjoyed another welcome visit from friends, this time from the north, who we used to go on motorcycle holidays with when we were all serious track day addicts. Roy, Andrea and Seb arrived in style on their motorbikes: a Yamaha 750 Temere and Honda CBR 1100 XX. We enjoyed a great afternoon reminiscing about our biking holidays and race tracks we had ridden in France and Spain, as well as the scrapes and exploits we got into. We also had lots to share about what we have all been doing in our lives over the past few years.

Monday morning September 12th saw us waiting for the No.4 bus to take us from Whitby to Staithes, a little tumbledown ex-fishing village just up the coast. The village was very quaint with narrow cobbled streets, a few cafés, pubs and galleries and a harbour that dries out completely at low tide. It lies on one side of Staithes beck and the Cleveland Way passes through, crossing the beck by way of a footbridge. Here, James Cook was apprenticed, age 16, to William Sanderson to work in his shop and it was William who then recommended him to John Walker in Whitby.

Updating on the weather in Staithes, we saw just a two-day window before strong northerly winds reaching force 6 or 7 (25-38 mph) were due to arrive. These winds were in the right direction for our sail southwards, but they would make Whitby entrance hazardous to leave and would also create a large sea swell, so we decided to cut short our visit to Whitby and sail south to anchor in Filey Bay, before heading down to Grimsby on our way to the Wash and our final destination, Fosdyke.

Whilst in Whitby I received two messages from campaign supporters saying that the RNLI had dog toy flying rings on sale on their website, this was not good news. One of the FoHS wardens had sent an excellent e-mail to the RNLI explaining very politely the danger of these types of rings to seals. I immediately backed this up with my own e-mail and sent it to the marketing manager. Later the same day I received a reply thanking me for my message and advising that the rings had already been removed from sale. Also, that the RNLI were committed to a biodegradable, solid design for next year. This is the quickest and most positive response I've ever had. I sent my heartfelt thanks to the RNLI of which we are, of course, members.

On the way back to the marina from Staithes I called into a Yorkshire Trading shop, as they had beach toys on sale. I thanked them for selling solid frisbees, which I saw on display, then noted they had a flimsy type of flying ring as well. The manageress showed concern about the plight of the seals but said she has to sell what they are sent by head office, though she did agree to let them know of the problem. Popping in to the tourist information centre I was hugely heartened to find that someone from Ravenscar Seal Group had been in recently and told them about the 'Love Seals' flying rings campaign. They were awaiting leaflets and posters from them. This was the first time the campaign had arrived before me!

We left Whitby when the swing bridge opened at 7am shortly after high water on Tuesday September 13th with a light northerly wind forecast, force 2-4. There was still a slight swell coming into the entrance but nothing like the maelstrom we encountered the previous Friday on our arrival. We enjoyed a leisurely motor sail, arriving at Filey in the early afternoon. Here, we found a lovely big sweep of a bay fringed by a sandy beach all the way round to Flamborough Head and the nature reserve of Bempton Cliffs. Anchoring off the attractive little seaside town we were protected from the wind by Filey Brigg, an outcrop of rocks, but there was a little swell coming in from the northeast which gave us a safe, but rolly night.

Flamborough Head projects well out into the North Sea and is another tidal gate, which means the streams run strongly around it. We arose early to catch the south flowing tide at the start of our long passage towards Grimsby, and were glad to move on after an uncomfortable night. The weather was fair and calm apart from the swell, which increased towards the head and lessened once we had passed it. The coast then became distant and low and the sea, already relatively shallow at 30 odd metres, reduced in depth to 20 then 15 metres, not a place to be in rough onshore weather as steeper waves are thrown up than in a deeper sea. Happily, today was calm and we passed inside Westernmost Rough wind farm and Humber Gateway wind farm without incident, as we neared Spurn Point at the north of the Humber Estuary.

The trick in this passage was timing our arrival at the estuary to coincide with the flood to take us in, negotiating the TSS which denotes the channel for commercial shipping and arriving at Grimsby when the locks were open in free flow. Consequently, we slowed down to make sure we arrived at the TSS at 16.30, radioed Humber Vessel Traffic Scheme (VTS), who monitored our passage and arrived at Grimsby half an hour before the locks opened at 19.00. As we neared Grimsby we noticed another sailing yacht, Ava, across the river which was also making for the harbour. We hoped we could follow them in as the entrance was difficult to make out, but they took time to approach and in the end we followed some smaller power boats. It was another Whitehills experience (the Scottish fishing port with a tiny, blind entrance) on a larger scale. The wind had picked up as we neared Grimsby making the river choppy and there was quite a current across the entrance to the open locks, we were glad to reach calm water inside Fish Docks where the little marina, run by Humber Cruising Association, has its home.

Grimsby was not at the top of our list of visitor destinations, but we actually received the friendliest welcome of the whole of our trip. As we arrived at the visitor pontoon a local couple from the Association took our lines and said the club house was open. Then Ava, the other yacht, arrived and the skipper invited us to join him and his crew in the club house. He took us under his wing and showed us how to order a take away to be delivered, along with theirs, to the club, the marina being some way from the town and not within easy walking distance.

Max, the skipper on Ava, had been a sailing instructor for many years, as well as working on one of the local dredgers and, in the past, for Humber VTS. He was normally based in Hull and was visiting Grimsby as Hull marina was closed for a couple of weeks whilst the locks were being maintained. He shared with us some of his local knowledge about the Humber, its shifting sand banks and tides and the East coast including the Wash. Boats can get caught out in the shallows of the river especially above the Humber bridge and he told us of one such incident where the unfortunate skipper ran aground on a sand bank and then insisted on staying on his boat for 10 days, until the tide was high enough to float him off! Friends took him supplies, though goodness knows how they reached him?! Max was naturally inclusive and generous – as well as looking after us he gave away half his chips to club members sitting at a table nearby.

We had got into the swing of being in a new town. Coming from the sea to an unknown place was like dropping out of the sky: we had no idea of what to expect, where to go and what to see. So, we had a look online at Grimsby's attractions and found: the National Fishing Heritage Centre, the Time Trap museum, and nearby, the Coastal Light Railway at Cleethorpes. We had already seen the first icon of Grimsby when we arrived: at the entrance of Grimsby harbour stands the impressive hydraulic accumulator Dock Tower, designed by the engineer James William Wild and completed in 1852. The tower used to contain a huge reservoir of water which provided the hydraulic power to work the locks and dock machinery and stands over 61 metres tall. The design was based on the Italian secular tower 'Torre del Mangia' in Siena and is visible for miles around. The power for the lock gates and machinery is now provided by electricity but this magnificent monument still stands tall at the lock entrance for all to see.

The National Fishing Heritage museum concentrated on the heyday of Great Grimsby as the world's busiest fishing port in the 1950s. Our tour started with the shrimper Perseverance, the last wooden sailing fishing boat to work from Grimsby, which had been beautifully renovated by a community group. We then entered a labyrinth of reconstructed areas representing a fishing trawler: the galley, the front of the boat where the crew slept and played games off watch, the steam boiler room where fires were stoked, the communications room, the bridge, and the deck which swayed to and fro as if on the sea! It was extremely well done, very atmospheric and quiet – we were on our own most of the time.

As we surfaced from deck level, a man was sitting nearby and we thought at first glance he was one of the exhibits. He then came to life, asking us how we were doing and added that he was an ex-trawler man himself, now working these past four years for the museum. He had sailed mainly in the North Sea but also as far as the Falkland Islands and explained his working life – spending three weeks at sea then a mere three days off to be with his family. The shifts were long, 18 hours followed by six hours of sleep, yet he enjoyed the life despite it being known as the most dangerous peacetime occupation.

The museum showed how important fishing was to Grimsby. The Royal Dock and Fish Docks were built and extended to shelter the boats and provide landing quays for the fish, many of which were transported by train down to Billingsgate market in London. Since the Cod Wars in the 1970s, when Iceland successfully expanded its fishing territory, keeping foreign vessels out, the problem of over fishing had gradually been recognised and became an issue of grave concern. From that time, the UK fishing industry declined, though the ex-trawler man we met explained how beam trawling continues to destroy the seabed, leaving a desert in its wake, and yet is still allowed.

Leaving the museum we walked through the town centre and called into the council offices to leave a seal campaign leaflet. We found the Town Hall was open to the public as it was heritage week in Grimsby. We were able to wander where we wished and also explored the Time Trap museum, capturing moments and buildings of the past couple of centuries in Great Grimsby. Here we found out how the name 'Grimsby' originated: an unwitting Viking merchant trader was used in the kidnap and planned murder of the Danish Prince Havelok in the 9th century. However, he befriended and saved the Prince instead, eventually landing in the marshes at Lindsey, the land that became his, and took his name Grim. The literal meaning is 'the settlement of Grim' and in Old Norse 'a foreboding place in the marshes'. The following day we took the bus to Cleethorpes and took a mini ride of one mile on the Coastal Light Railway to enjoy the beginning of their Blues Festival at Lakeside station.

*

I had been keen to pop into the Council offices in Grimsby as we were back on the East coast and there is a big seal colony at Donna Nook just outside the mouth of the Humber estuary. The Norfolk coastal councils, as I mentioned earlier, had given valuable support to the campaign. I had heard of one councillor, Tim Adams, who was voicing concern about the seals getting caught in the rings and when I contacted him he arranged for Peter and myself to give a presentation to Cromer Town Council's Planning and Environment Committee in September 2019. This was my first experience of public speaking and I was nervous! I took my notes and a number of photos, showing seals caught in plastic flying rings, which I had got enlarged. When I started to show them they fell out of my hands in a heap on the floor! Despite this, we explained the problem and the councillors responded well, they were keen to help. They sent a funding application which resulted in £500 being awarded to FoHS to support the campaign and one councillor said he felt there should be an outright ban on the rings.

In that first year I also gave presentations to the North Norfolk District Council, (NNDC), Coastal Forum and to the Borough Council of King's Lynn and West Norfolk's (BCKLWN) Environment and Community Panel. NNDC followed up with their 'Safer Seals' campaign highlighting key messages: not to throw flying rings on the beach, keeping dogs on leads and staying a good distance from the seals. The following year, 2020, King's Lynn Environment Panel put a proposal forward to ban the use of flying rings on their beaches in order to protect the seals.

I was also invited to give a presentation in September 2021 to the Environment Committee of Great Yarmouth Borough Council. They also gave great support and decided to try and become a flying ring-free town as well as proposing a ban on the rings to the Secretary of State for Defra (Department for Environment, Food and Rural Affairs).

*

15

Homeward Bound to The Wash

SEPTEMBER 18TH, 2022

On Sunday September 18th we provisioned up for the final time and treated ourselves by going to Sainsbury's in Grimsby. Most of the time we had only had access to little supermarkets near the harbours, which are generally limited in their range of food especially vegetarian options. Greengrocers with unpackaged fruit and veg and wholefood shops had been rare and cherished when we discovered them. We had bought much more packaged food than we do at home and always looked for recycling facilities where we stopped. The quality of these had varied a lot around the country but at the Association's marina they were very good. I had also started to save plastic marked 'unrecyclable' to put in our TerraCycle zero waste box when we reached home.

We were invited to join club members to watch the Queen's funeral procession and service on the clubhouse TV the next day and found it impressive, sad and moving, just as the other millions, I'm sure, who were there or watching. All those people lining the streets to watch her hearse pass by were truly amazing to see. We then enjoyed the delicious spread that the members had prepared, including roast potatoes, sausages and a selection of vegetarian dishes.

After checking the weather we decided to leave on the Wednesday when light winds veering from south to southwest and little swell were forecast. We also had to fit in our 66 mile passage with the opening of the lock gates at Grimsby, the ebb tide to take us out of the Humber and a flood tide to enter the Wash and, if possible, take us all the way up the river Welland to Fosdyke Yacht Haven, Spirit's winter home. So, on Tuesday evening we went early to bed as we had only four hours to sleep before rising at 2am to pass through the locks at 3am. Richard managed some kip, I don't think I slept a wink, I was on high alert thinking about navigating for 3 hours out of the Humber in the dark.

Ships are working 24/7 on the Humber and the docks and river were busy next morning. As we radioed Fish Dock Island to gain permission to leave the harbour we were told to standby whilst a ship manoeuvred outside the lock. We then set off motoring Spirit in very little wind on course for our first buoy Lower Burcom, a red port hand mark flashing red every 4 seconds. This is how buoys marking the channel are identified at night: by their coloured light sequence. The flashes were not easy to pick out against the myriad of other lights on shore, on other boats, buoys and marks, but gradually we gained our night vision and saw the four second red flashes. I find it quite unnerving sailing at night, when it's totally dark with no moonlight and I was looking forward to the dawn and being able to see again.

The chart plotter and AIS helped hugely, we could identify big ships in the main channel, a fishing vessel which came up behind and overtook us and a pilot boat who called us on the radio to check where we were heading. We hopped from buoy to buoy down the river and eventually the shipping disappeared and the final buoys of the estuary were reached as dawn started to reveal the grey shapes of gentle waves all around us. Wonderful, we could see again and were well on our way.

The rest of our passage to the Wash was uneventful. After dawn, I collapsed below for a welcome sleep, then swapped lookout duties with Richard. We both find motoring a bit tedious compared to sailing, but the discovery of audio books and podcasts has greatly enlivened our experience. I listened to 'The Butterfly Isles' by Patrick Barkham whilst Richard slept. We made the Wash at last and could just make out the white tower of Hunstanton lighthouse in the hazy distance. We knew our village lay further along the coast and it was unbelievable to think our home was actually across there.

The Wash is like a huge estuary or collection of estuaries with one deep channel running through the middle and a number of smaller ones reaching out like fingers from the rivers. In between the channels lie sandbanks, habitats for wildlife including colonies of harbour seals (the Wash having the largest population in Europe), as well as being treacherous to boats, especially in heavy onshore weather. Today, the weather gods were kind and all we had to concentrate on was finding the right buoys to take us through Freeman Channel, on towards Tabs Head, the junction for the Haven River to Boston and the River Welland for Fosdyke. We had the tide with us and it was still on the rise, so if we did touch the bottom we would soon float again, also our timing was perfect for continuing right on up to the little boatyard.

The Welland is blessed with wildlife: we saw groups of harbour seals hauled out, egrets, cormorants and a variety of waders including oyster catchers. A space had been prepared for us on one of the two river pontoons at Fosdyke and Richard turned Spirit to face into the flooding tide which was carrying us, at some speed, towards the very low road bridge over the A17! We were home and almost dry, or so we assumed.

Although we thought we had depth on the pontoon for Spirit, Richard suggested we needed to double check, especially as springs, with the greatest range of tide, was approaching. I started to look at the figures but these were not adding up for me, so I begged a nap and left Richard to do the tide calculations based on the heights at Tabs Head. When I awoke, he said I would not like what he had found: the upshot was that on the next day we would ground a little and then it would get much worse. Over the weekend Spirit would be high and dry by up to a metre risking her falling over. We were due to be lifted out the following week, when there was enough depth of water at high tide in the lifting bay, so we would have to go back out into the Wash and anchor until then! For the second time in our voyage, I held my head in my hands and I admit to some ranting and railing. I had been so happy and relieved that we had made Fosdyke without any major mishaps and thought we could now relax and enjoy our homecoming: this had all apparently been a mirage.

On Thursday, we looked again and again at the figures, dug out our traditional lead line from the back of a cupboard and took soundings around the boat. At low water we found that there appeared to be more water at the pontoon compared with the predicted tidal height at Tabs Head, probably due to the fresh water continually flowing down the river. However, if the level continued to drop over the next few days we would still be in trouble. Whilst the optimal day for lifting was on the highest spring tide the following week, when there would be plenty of depth of water in the lifting bay, the yard helpfully agreed to see if they could lift us out that evening.

We worked quickly to prepare Spirit taking down the genoa sail and shortly before high tide accompanied the boat yard manager in his work boat to help him take soundings in the lifting bay and its approach. It looked as if we might just have enough depth, two metres, apart from one spot. We decided to give it a go and reverse out if necessary.

The next half hour was tense: soon after 5pm, Richard motored Spirit to the waiting pontoon next to the lifting bay, keeping close in to the pontoon to stay in the deeper water. Then, with the engine off, he and I stepped ashore and, taking a line each fore and aft, pulled our boat towards the bay whilst the manager worked the hoist: lowering the two slings that would hold Spirit as she was lifted out of the water. She gradually slipped over the slings without faltering, as we held our breath, and after manoeuvring them into place the manager started to lift them: nine tons of boat rose high into the air and for the first time we had been hands on helping. It was a huge relief for us all that the lift was successful. At last we could start to relax.

We boarded Spirit using one of the yard ladders and spent a comfortable night suspended in the slings as Spirit's metal cradle had not arrived. Some boats, such as bilge keelers which have two keels, are able to take the ground, which means they can safely dry out, balanced on their keels, without falling over. Those such as Spirit, which have a single keel, need strong support, such as a steel cradle, to keep them upright when out of the water. At Fosdyke, most people owned their own cradle and Richard had ordered one to be made especially for Spirit. This had been due to arrive on Wednesday or Thursday, then we heard it would come at lunchtime on Friday, a bit tight now that she was out of the water! The last hurdle was still to be leapt, would it arrive in time for the manager to move Spirit into her winter quarters, freeing up the travel hoist, before the weekend when all work would cease? Richard called the cradle company in the morning and was reassured the courier was on his way and at 11am the cradle duly arrived but in flat pack form with no instructions! Thankfully, the manager helped us put it all together, manoeuvred the hoist into place and gently started to lower Spirit down. Her hull fitted beautifully into the purpose built cradle, snugly held by six support pads. At long last and after much anxiety on all sides, now we could really relax. During those two fraught days there had been moments of joy such as when we saw a flash of iridescent turquoise pass very swiftly down the inside of the pontoon and then a second: it was a pair of kingfishers who live on the river.

Having no car at Fosdyke, we had arranged for our friend Bridget to fetch us, so we hurriedly packed overnight bags and were whisked off that Friday afternoon of September 23rd to our shore based home just outside King's Lynn. We were very pleased to see that grass everywhere was green and our garden had survived the drought. We re-homed a

Spirit secure in her cradle, Fosdyke

number of spiders, hoovered the house and then enjoyed hot baths, a blissful luxury, before collapsing into bed.

So, we came to the time when our adventures for the year were complete and we were looking forward to our winter shore leave. I would be able to catch up with Hilda and Richard of FoHS who had been kindly holding the fort with the campaign over the summer. We had successfully sailed 1700 miles spending around 10 weeks, equally split, between being at anchor and on mooring buoys, with almost the same number of nights in marinas or harbours. Fuel costs were almost three times what we had budgeted for. We had been on a steep learning curve, enjoyed a fabulous time on our six month adventure and now had many, many experiences to savour.

*

I'll finish with another true story.

Out for the day on the North Norfolk coast, near the start of the campaign, I was watching a group of seals, from a good distance, some of which were hauled out on rocks above the beach. The seals were resting and relaxing, occasionally one would yawn showing its pink mouth and sharp, white teeth. They resembled huge pebbles with an array of mottled colours in shades of brown and grey through to almost black. I felt a deep affinity for them. Then, as I watched, it dawned on me that seals have their own lives, social groups and relationships. At best, as a human, I might arouse some curiosity in them at worst, fear of disturbance or aggression. I knew my responsibility was, and is, to do all I can to enable seals to continue to live in their own world in peace – from us.

I may mean nothing to seals but they, and the natural environment they are part of, mean the world to me.

*

Pinkafo released on Horsey Beach with her neck wound still visible (Photo by Chris Godfrey RIP)

Epilogue

Relaxing on my comfy sofa at home on the afternoon of Tuesday November 15th 2022 someone from Radio Norfolk rang me asking if I would be happy to speak on the breakfast show the next morning about the seals and flying rings. I replied, 'yes of course, but why now?' The reason was to do with the proposal by King's Lynn Environment Panel to ban flying rings, but they were not sure what stage it had reached.

I quickly contacted the council and found out that Cabinet, the executive wing, was meeting in a couple of hours' time and the proposed ban was on the agenda! After a nail-biting few hours I was able to look at the recording of the meeting on the council's YouTube channel and scroll through to the right agenda item. As I listened to the councillors discussing the proposed ban on flying rings alongside an enhanced ban on sky lanterns and helium balloons my heart started to lift: they were very concerned about the injuries being caused to seals by flying rings, also to land animals from the lanterns and balloons.

Cabinet resolved:

'That the use of flying rings on council beaches be prohibited and their use be proactively discouraged in other areas where there is a chance they could end up in the sea.'

(From the Cabinet's draft minutes
of November 15th 2022)

My heart soared! This was the first council in the UK to ban flying rings! It was a huge step forward, a precedent which hopefully other councils first in Norfolk then further afield would follow. I prepared for my live talk on Radio Norfolk and delivered it next morning with renewed vigour along with huge thanks to the council.

A feature on the ban with footage of Evangelos Achilleos, manager of RSPCA East Winch Wildlife Centre, was aired on national television by BBC1 Breakfast on November 21st. Evangelos gave an excellent explanation of how seals were getting caught and injured in plastic flying rings and how pleased he and the RSPCA were that the council had taken positive action to ban them on their beaches.

However on further reading of the Cabinet's minutes I saw:

'That it be acknowledged that the extent of powers available currently are to warn, inform and engage with land users in the hope they comply, currently there are no associated resource to patrol the affected areas nor powers to penalise anyone failing to comply.'

The ban was a good start but the challenge of establishing a robust legal framework remained.

Keeping Seals Safe
from plastic flying rings

You can help by~

- Telling your family and friends about the seals and how they can get caught in flying rings

- Sharing the plight of the seals entangled in flying rings with your friends and contacts through social media

- Talking to shops selling flying rings and showing them a photo of an entangled seal from this book or on your phone. Suggest seal-safe solid frisbees instead, biodegradable ones are even better – please be friendly!

- Taking a bag to collect litter when you visit the beach, a litter picker makes it fun and easier to do!

- Getting creative, making posters, getting schools involved, telling groups you are in about the seals

**Please don't throw flying rings on the beach,
in the sea or near waterways**

Watch Seals Safely – 5 Golden Rules

◆ Respect that seals are easily disturbed by the presence of humans. Never ever get close to a seal – if they look at you they are already stressed. Seals are wild animals and have a very painful bite

◆ If you have a dog with you always keep the dog on a lead and away from seals

◆ Stay off beaches when seals are pupping. Never get between a mother and her pup – she may abandon it

◆ Never encourage a seal back in the water they may drown

◆ If you come across a seal on a beach it will be there for a reason. It could be resting or waiting for its coat to moult. Alternatively it may be unwell or injured. If you have concerns get in touch with the RSPCA, BDMLR or a voluntary seal group in the area

Seals are protected by law – it is illegal to harm them in the UK all year round
(Conservation of Seals Act 1970 and Fisheries Act 2021)

(A private member's bill submitted by Tracey Crouch to make it an offence to intentionally or recklessly disturb or harass a seal is currently waiting for its second reading in parliament.)

Useful Seal Contacts and Information

If you come across a seal that is injured or in distress:

RSPCA hotline (England and Wales)	0300 1234 999
SSPCA hotline (Scotland)	03000 999 999
BDMLR hotline (British Divers Marine Life Rescue)	01825 765546
FOHS hotline (Friends of Horsey Seals, Norfolk)	07706 314 514

Websites

www.friendsofhorseyseals.co.uk for seal information and becoming a volunteer warden in Norfolk

www.rspca.org.uk and **www.scottishspca.org** for information on animal welfare and becoming a volunteer

www.bdmlr.org.uk for information on seals, other marine mammals, rescues and becoming a volunteer

www.sealresearchtrust.com previously Cornwall Seal Group Research Trust for information about seals, how to report seal sightings and becoming a seal supporter

www.sealalliance.org links for all the main seal groups in the UK and Ireland working to protect seals, a wealth of media resources including the 'Watching Seals Well' poster

Campaign coverage online links:

https://www.itv.com/news/anglia/2019-07-24/
campaign-launched-after-heartbreaking-cases-of-seals-
trapped-in-plastic-rings

https://www.itv.com/news/anglia/2020-08-10/norfolk-
seal-sculpture-created-to-warn-beachgoers-of-dangers-of-
plastic-toys

https://www.bbc.co.uk/news/av/uk-england-
norfolk-62325934 'Seal Supporter sails around Britain for
flying rings awareness'.

https://www.bbc.co.uk/newsround/63702681 'Ring
frisbees banned on Norfolk beaches to protect seals' also

Article 'A Hole lot of Trouble' by Hannah Parry, Norfolk
Magazine December 2022 Issue

Bibliography

Reeds Nautical Almanac 2022 Atlantic Europe
Bloomsbury Publishing
ISBN: 9781399402552

The Shell Channel Pilot by Tom Cunliffe
Eighth Edition 2021, Published by Imray Laurie Norie and
Wilson Ltd
ISBN: 9781846237003

West Country Cruising Companion by Mark Fishwick
Published 2004 by Nautical Data Ltd ISBN: 190435825X

Isles of Scilly RCC Pilot by Graham Adam
Fifth Edition 2010, Published by Imray Laurie Norie and
Wilson Ltd
ISBN: 9780852888506

Lundy and Irish Sea Pilot by David Taylor Second Edition
2001, Published by Imray Laurie Norie and Wilson Ltd
ISBN: 0852884486

East and North Coasts of Ireland Sailing Directions by
Irish Cruising Club
Ninth Edition 1999, Published by Irish Cruising Club
Publications Ltd
ISBN: 0950171786

The Scottish Islands, a Guide to Every Scottish Island by Hamish Haswell-Smith 2015 Edition, Published by Canongate Books
ISBN: 9781782116783

Firth of Clyde Sailing Directions and Anchorages by Clyde Cruising Club
Second Edition 2016, Published by Imray Laurie Norie and Wilson Ltd
ISBN: 9781846236983

Clyde to Colonsay the Yachtsman's Pilot, by Martin Lawrence Third Edition 2001, Published by Imray Laurie Norie and Wilson Ltd
ISBN: 0852885067

Isle of Mull the Yachtsman's Pilot by Martin Lawrence Published 1999 by Imray Laurie Norie and Wilson Ltd
ISBN: 0852884044

Kintyre to Ardnamurchan Sailing Directions and Anchorages by Clyde Cruising Club 2014, Published by Imray Laurie Norie and Wilson Ltd
ISBN: 9781846235801

The Yachtsman's Pilot, Skye and Northwest Scotland by Martin Lawrence
Third Edition 2010, Published by Imray Laurie Norie and Wilson Ltd
ISBN: 9781846231780

Outer Hebrides Sailing Directions and Anchorages by Clyde Cruising Club
Second Edition, Published by Imray Laurie Norie and Wilson Ltd
ISBN: 9781846239038

Humber to Rattray Head Sailing Directions by Royal Northumberland Yacht Club, published by RNYC Fifth Edition 2002
ISBN: 0951599712

Tidal Havens of The Wash and Humber by Henry Irving Sixth Edition 2011, Published by Imray Laurie Norie and Wilson Ltd
ISBN: 9781846232794

United Kingdom Hydrographic Office (UKHO)
Admiralty Standard Nautical Charts

UKHO Leisure Folios

UKHO Admiralty Tidal Stream Atlas (various regions)

Imray Nautical Charts

Navionics Platinum+ Digital Chart for our Raymarine Electronic Chart Plotter
United Kingdom, Ireland and Holland

Antares Digital Charts for the West Coast of Scotland
Supplementary very large-scale digital charts of UKHO cartography
Available at: **www.antarescharts.co.uk**

Cruising Association App CAptain's Mate, available to members website: **www.theca.org.uk**

Weather and sea state sites:
Shipping and inshore waters forecast
www.metoffice.co.uk
WaveNet interactive map **www.cefas.co.uk**
Windy.app
www.xcweather.co.uk also XCWeather app

Acknowledgements

My thanks go to all our friends, family, neighbours and work colleagues who journeyed with us on Spirit by reading my blog. The positive feedback in your comments gave me the inspiration and encouragement to attempt the transformation of the blog into this book. I also sincerely thank the huge number of people who have supported the awareness campaign 'Keeping seals safe from plastic flying rings', please continue to do so.

My deep felt thanks go to all the trustees of FoHS in particular Peter Ansell who has given me unconditional encouragement from day one; Albert Ward who has worked tirelessly with me on publicity, liaison and keeping the campaign alive through his eloquent website reports, as well as writing the foreword for this book and checking my manuscript; David Vyse and Jane Bowden for linking the campaign into the media through their contacts and successful press releases; Hilda Stephenson for helping with the initial funding bids, promoting the campaign through the summers based at the FoHS Education Unit which she runs, and holding the fort for the campaign together with Richard Edwards, Duty Warden, whilst I was sailing around the country. Also Teresa and Billy Le Compte and Sally Butler who turned up in all weathers to support the campaign in action.

I thank the FoHS wardens who patrol the beaches all winter, and some during the summer, to protect the seals and talk to the public. Many of them, including Angela, Marilyn, Nikki, Caroline and Jean have taken the campaign to heart by distributing leaflets, talking to shops and beach visitors and supporting the Sealy beach tours. I am very grateful to wardens Lorraine Auton who painted the iconic seal image for the campaign and Tony Colledge who designed the original poster and has given his time freely and promptly to provide an array of magnificent updates.

Huge thanks go to all at the RSPCA East Winch Wildlife Centre including the previous manager Alison Charles and present manager Evangelos Achilleos, the vets, vet nurses, wildlife assistants and volunteers who care for the seals and all the wild animal patients all day every day to give them every chance of recovery and a successful release.

So many other groups and people have given their time enthusiastically and passionately to the campaign including: Sea-Changers who funded our publicity; Dan Goldsmith of Marine and Wildlife Rescue, Norfolk; Di Westwood, Jo Collins and Julia Cable from BDMLR who have distributed publicity and included the plight of the seals caught in flying rings in their school talks; Sue Sayer and members of the Seal Research Trust in Cornwall who have developed an amazing resources file for the campaign; groups from the Seal Alliance including Gareth Richards of the Gower Seal Group; Ann and Matt from the Marine Conservation Society; Nathan Barnett and his staff at Great Yarmouth Sealife; Callum Browett of the International Otter Survival Fund; and Kate Wing, who started a petition calling for a ban on flying rings to protect the seals. I thank you all.

Special gratitude goes to Gaywood Valley Conservation Group of which I am a member. Chair, Michael de Whalley who is also a Green Party councillor and member of the Environment Panel, encouraged me and promoted the campaign within King's Lynn Council; John Hayes who leads the group took the message to his local Cubs group and distributed publicity along with Brian Hillman; Viv West joined me on the Sealy tour. Others have spread the message and given interest and encouragement to the campaign.

Councillors from the BCKLWN, NNDC and GYBC as well as many from the Parish councils have supported the campaign and are working to protect the seals. Special thanks go to members of the King's Lynn Environment Panel including Carol Bower, Anthony Bubb, Terry Parish also Colin Rose; Tim Adams, leader of NNDC who has been a strong supporter from the start; and members of GYBC Environment Committee especially Paul Wells Chair, Barbara Wright and Kerry Robinson Payne members. Also to Karen Youngs of the Great Yarmouth Tourism and Business Area.

I am very grateful to all the teachers who engaged so many of their pupils in completing project work on the campaign, and to the children who expressed such heartfelt sympathy and understanding for the seals.

I deeply thank my friend Bridget Villatoro who set up my blog website with Glen Jobson and has acted as a sounding board, fellow Sealy display tourer and link to Becka Elliot who we assisted in sculpting the amazing Sealy. To friends: Nicky Rowland who was one of our main blog supporters and gave valuable advice on my book manuscript; and Hilary Clark who diligently proof read the manuscript.

I give huge thanks to my sisters Clare, Phil and Sue for keeping me company through my blog and for all their help with the campaign including; their enthusiastic support and ideas; providing funding for the hi-vis campaign vests; joining me to distribute publicity and talk to people about the seals; and joining FoHS.

Finally my deepest thanks go to my husband Richard who has provided invaluable advice and boosted my confidence when I most needed it. He accompanied me on my first campaign trips and has provided an ongoing positive sounding board. His sailing, technical and engineering skills made our sailing adventure possible, his vision and hard work made it happen.